ABANDONED WESTERN PENNSYLVANIA

BEHIND THE BOARDS

KARI MILLER

AMERICA
THROUGH TIME®
ADDING COLOR TO AMERICAN HISTORY

America Through Time is an imprint of Fonthill Media LLC
www.through-time.com
office@through-time.com

Published by Arcadia Publishing by arrangement with Fonthill Media LLC
For all general information, please contact Arcadia Publishing:
Telephone: 843-853-2070
Fax: 843-853-0044
E-mail: sales@arcadiapublishing.com
For customer service and orders:
Toll-Free 1-888-313-2665

www.arcadiapublishing.com

First published 2023

ISBN 978-1-63499-484-2

Typeset in Trade Gothic 10pt on 15pt
Printed and bound in England

CONTENTS

PREFACE

I have always had a healthy curiosity when it comes to abandoned and derelict places. Sometimes these places remain untouched and almost frozen in time. Other times they are empty, leaving nothing but the mystery of who once occupied the structure and why they left. That is the question that I am asked most often: why they left, why is this place abandoned?

I am not entirely sure what attracts me to abandoned spaces so intently, but I do know where it all started. I grew up in a small town in New Jersey—the kind of small town that had had one post office for the whole town, and everyone had a P.O. box. So small even that all the grades, kindergarten through twelfth grade, shared the same bus. Around the corner from my home sat an abandoned school. One night, my mom and my stepdad thought they would scare us by driving around the half circle drive in front of the school, all the while telling us a terrifying story of a headmaster who used to beat the children and that is why the school shut down. To this day, I am not sure if that story is actually true or not.

It was soon after that night that me and my stepbrother, Scott, snuck down to the school. We rode our bikes so that we could get away quickly if we needed. We snuck around the back of the school and dropped them in the grass. The playground was still there but was overgrown and lost in the foliage. I remember the descent down the staircase that led to the school's basement. We did not have flashlights, nor did we have any idea what we were doing. I was only in second grade at the time. Being in grade school might have been the initial infatuation with the school.

We made our way up to the first floor. I will never forget the smell. For those of you who have never ventured inside an abandoned place, it is hard to explain the smell, but I will try. It is a smell that you can taste, a smell of stale air, of rot. Lack of air circulation and water damage creates a unique aroma. It gets even worse if there is furniture and carpeting left behind.

I wish that I could say I remember the place in explicit detail, but I was young. I remember cobwebs, the creaky floors, dust, and the smell. I remember being terrified and excited all at once. We came upon a room that had desks lined up the way most traditional classrooms are set up. There were books on the desks as if the students could return at any time. The empty classrooms, untouched and undisturbed for years, fascinated me. I cannot tell you how many times we snuck back into the school; I just know it was a weekly occurrence.

I moved away a few years later and said goodbye to my dilapidated playground, but I did not say goodbye to the curiosity, trading one abandoned school for many different kinds of abandonments. In high school, I took over five photography classes: something about capturing moments, people, and places was incredible to me. I had the ability to freeze time, to create a permanent memory. It was not long before I was taking photos of everything.

A few years after graduating high school, I returned to my hometown to find the school was now an empty field. I do not have a single photograph of it, which leads me to why I take photos of abandoned locations, why for me, it is more than just a hobby or an adventure now. It is a piece of history that I can preserve in photographs. People today and generations after will know these homes, buildings, and places once existed.

More importantly, I can share with the world what I have seen—what lies behind the boards.

ABOUT THE AUTHOR

Kari Miller has been a photographer for over ten years. She began exploring abandoned locations since elementary school. She grew up in a very small town and would often sneak into the town's abandoned school. Since a young age, her desire to explore abandoned locations has only grown. In high school, she was introduced to photography and learned both film and digital photography. She then began photographing abandoned locations while she explored them. Kari has travelled all over the East Coast and the Midwest regions of the United States, exploring an abundance of locations. Kari loves taking pictures, collecting history, and observing what people have left behind.

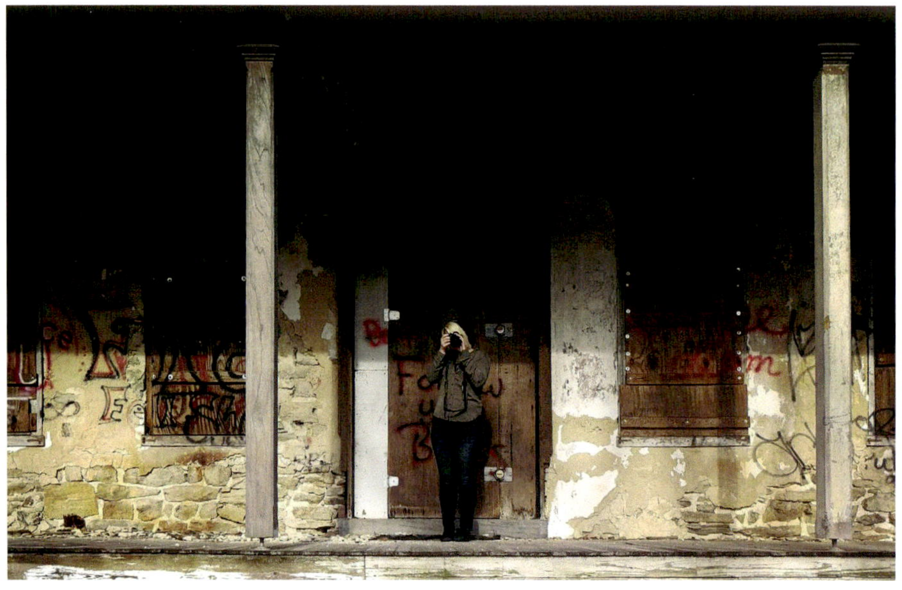

INTRODUCTION

Pennsylvania was once the heartland of steel production and coal mining. During World War II, American steel mills made more than half of the world's steel. After the war, there was a global demand for steel, and the demand for new cars was also great. Efficient processes such as oxygen furnaces and continuous casters led to the decline in jobs as less manpower was needed. Western Pennsylvania saw substantial job loss during the 1950s. Millions lost their jobs in the 1970s through the 1980s due to plant closings. There was massive unemployment; by 1979, half of the workers were let go. The steel industry in Western PA completely collapsed in the 1980s. Western Pennsylvania has not had as much success in rebuilding as Eastern Pennsylvania has after deindustrialization. Job loss and population decreases have led to poverty and an increase in abandoned structures.

1

BROWNSVILLE GENERAL HOSPITAL

In the early 1900s in Brownsville, Pennsylvania, you had to travel to Fairmont or McKeesport if you were seeking medical care. There was no hospital in Brownsville; many people died waiting at the railroad station for transportation to neighboring hospitals. Coal mining had a strong presence in Brownsville, so the need for a hospital was at an all-time high. Along with Rev. E. M. Bowman, locals and medical professionals secured a charter for a hospital in 1910. The group earned $10,000 in fundraising. That same year, the Brownsville Public School was demolished, leaving an empty lot at the corner of Fifth Avenue and Church Street. The charter purchased the lot to be the new site of the Brownsville General Hospital.

According to local news sources, the hospital opened to the public in 1914, even though it was incomplete. In 1916, the hospital construction was complete, and a surgical ward was added. The hospital was constructed out of 4-foot buff-colored pressed face brick. The hospital consists of several units in a T-shape with right and left wings on a 45-degree angle to the center. The center building is two stories with a basement and a third-floor penthouse. The center building is where administration offices, x-ray, laboratory, and private hospital rooms were located. The rear building was two stories with a basement and contained the operating ward and boiler room. The left and right wings consisted of patient rooms, supply closets, and bathrooms. The hospital could treat 100 patients at a time comfortably. In 1920, the hospital established its own school of nursing. Then in 1926, Joseph H. Horner willed a large amount of money to the hospital. This donation led to the construction of a nurses' home directly across from the hospital on the opposite side of Church Street and Fifth Avenue. In 1965, the hospital moved to a new location. The old hospital was purchased by Frank Bock, who turned the hospital into the Golden Age

Age Nursing Home, a long-term care facility for the elderly. In 1984, a federal survey was conducted at the facility. The survey found severe violations and deficiencies. These violations terminated the Medicare agreement with the Golden Age Nursing Home. This terminated their license and reimbursement from Medicare. All new admissions to the facility were suspended. The Golden Age closed in 1984 after failing to come recertified with Medicare. The hospital has sat empty, unused, and deteriorating ever since. Today, where the hospital once stood is an open field. The demolition of the hospital was completed in early 2021.

Brownsville General Hospital was one of my favorite locations. Sadly, in its final years, the hospital had been significantly vandalized. I was lucky enough to see the hospital when it was mostly untouched by anyone but Mother Nature. Patient records were still in the file room, patient beds and bedpans were set up as if the patients would return at any moment, and supplies were still in the closets. The hospital was incredibly dangerous as much of the second floor was in the basement, and the floors grew weaker as each year passed. That did not stop me from wanting to explore every corridor of the place.

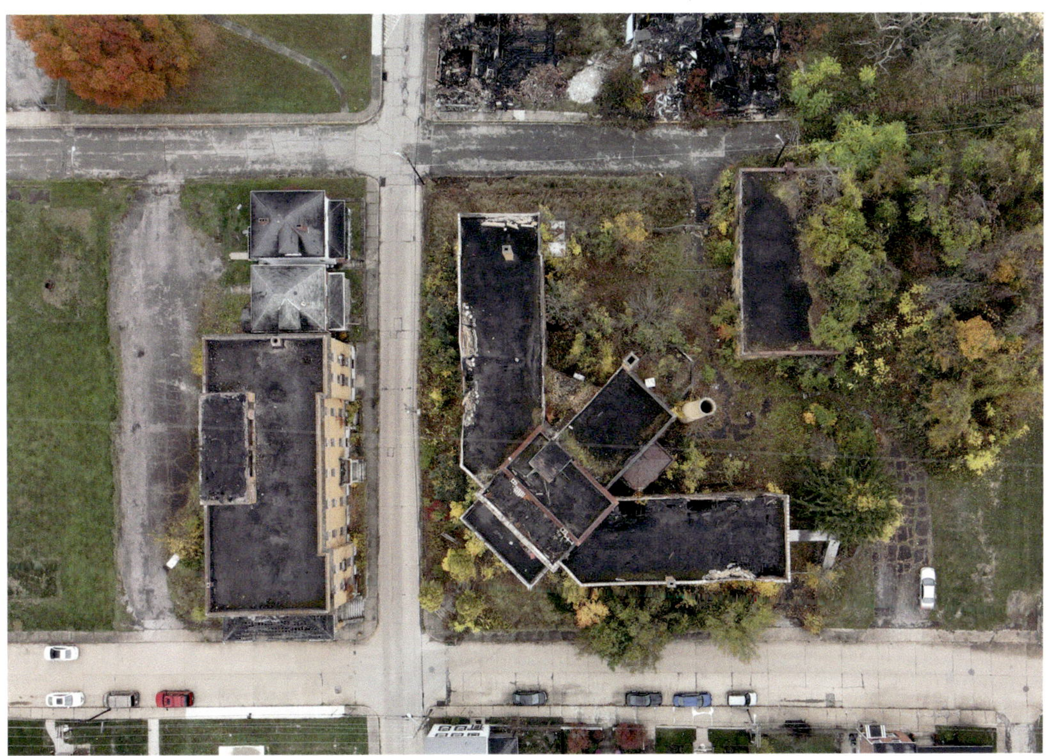

A drone shot of the Brownsville Hospital (right) and the Horner's Nurse Home (left).

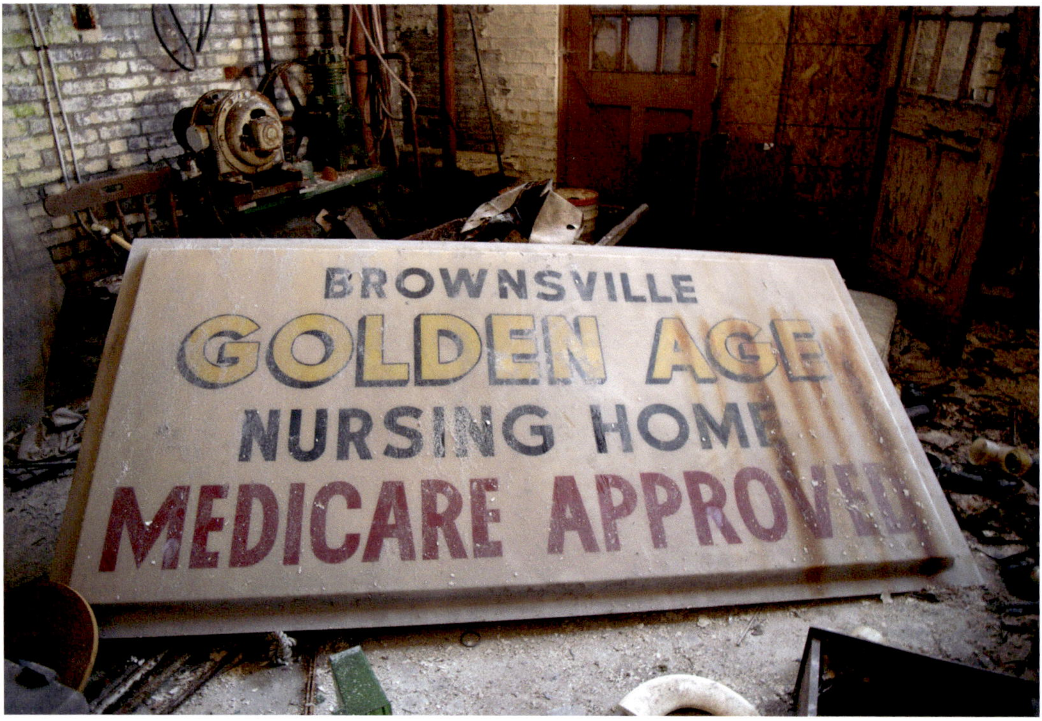

The old sign for the hospital was hidden away in what appeared to be an old maintenance building.

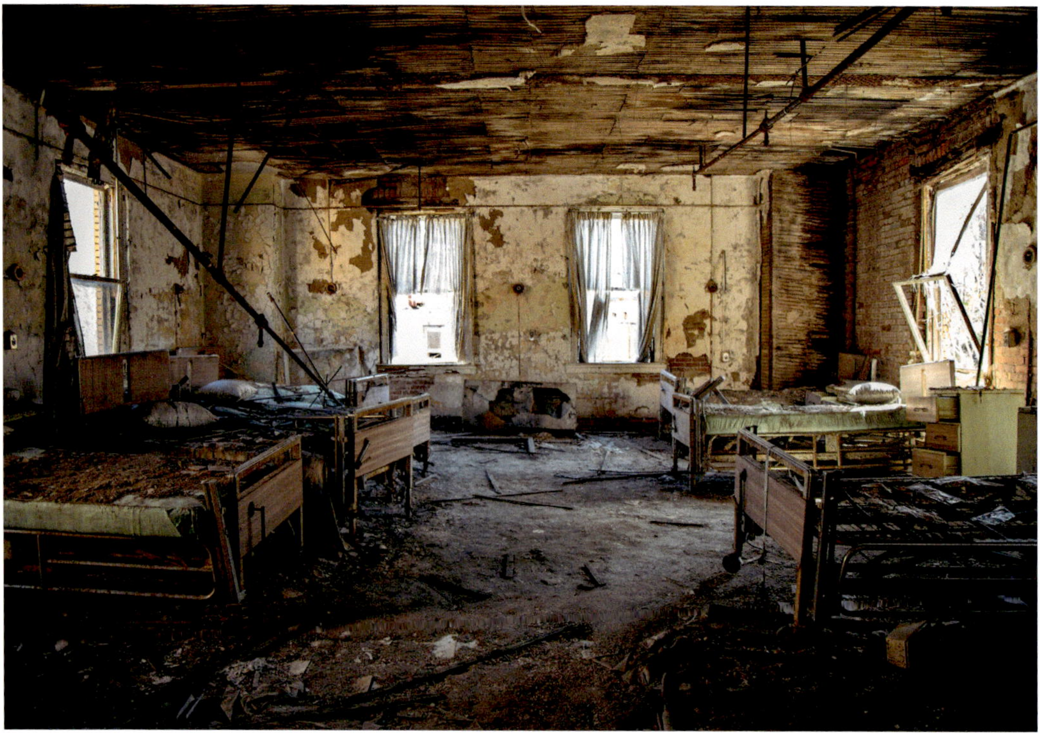

Hospital beds still lined the room.

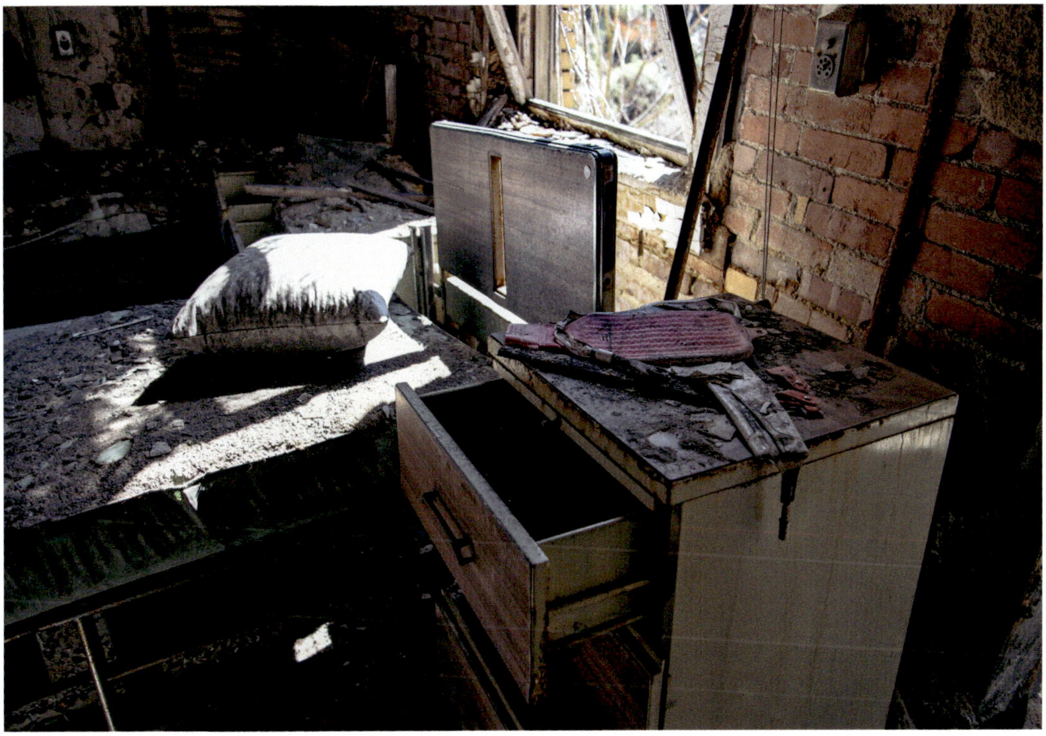

Pillows still on each bed and medical equipment remain long after the hospital closed.

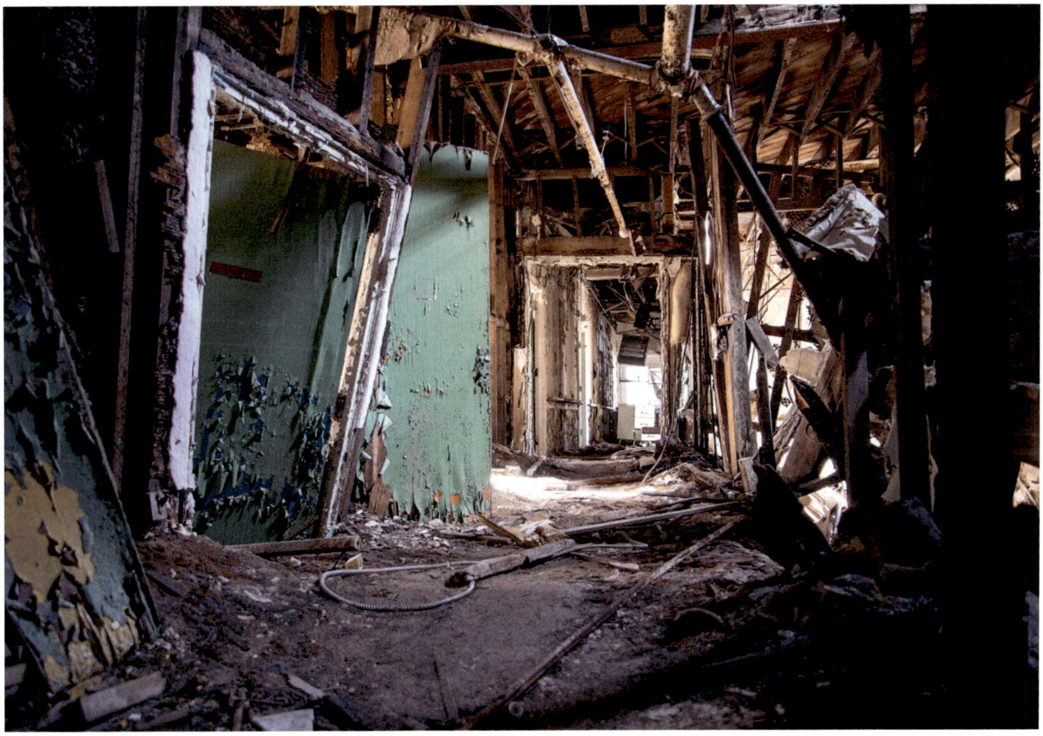

Doorways bending under the weight of the caving floor above.

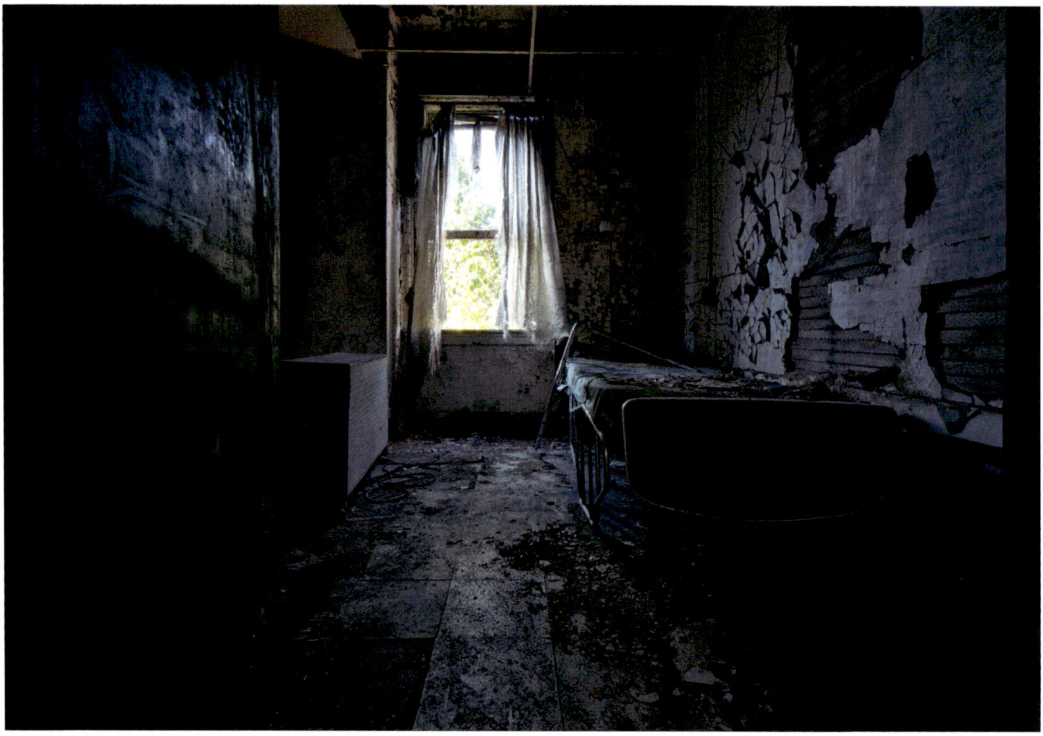

An early morning light illuminated one of the patient rooms.

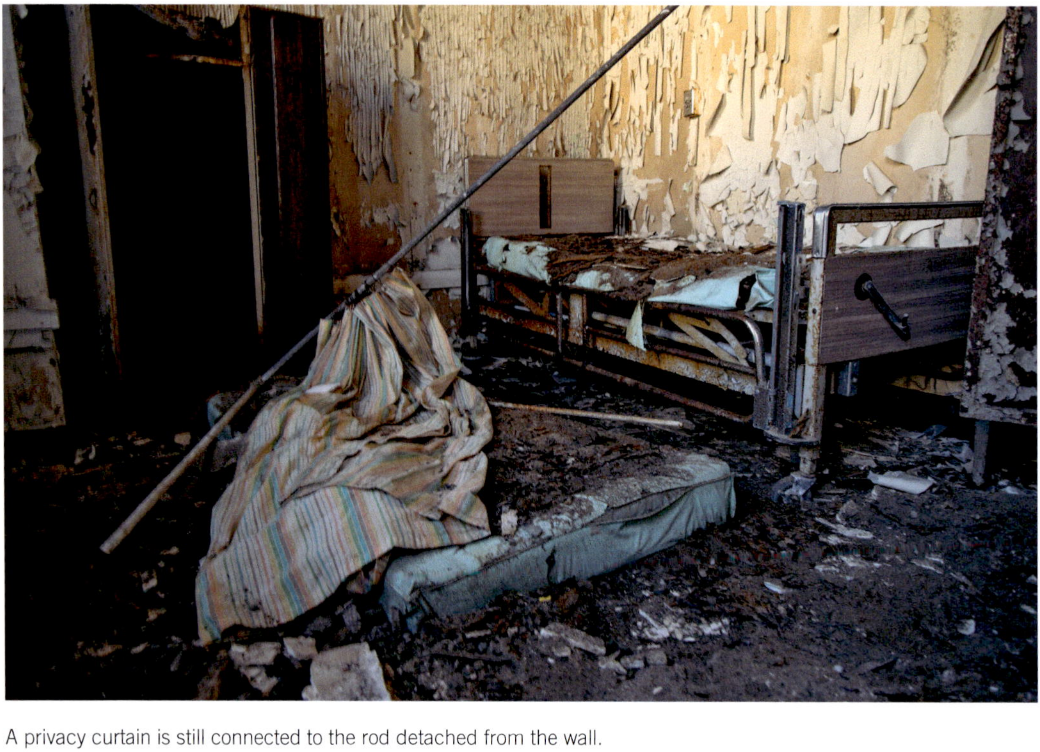

A privacy curtain is still connected to the rod detached from the wall.

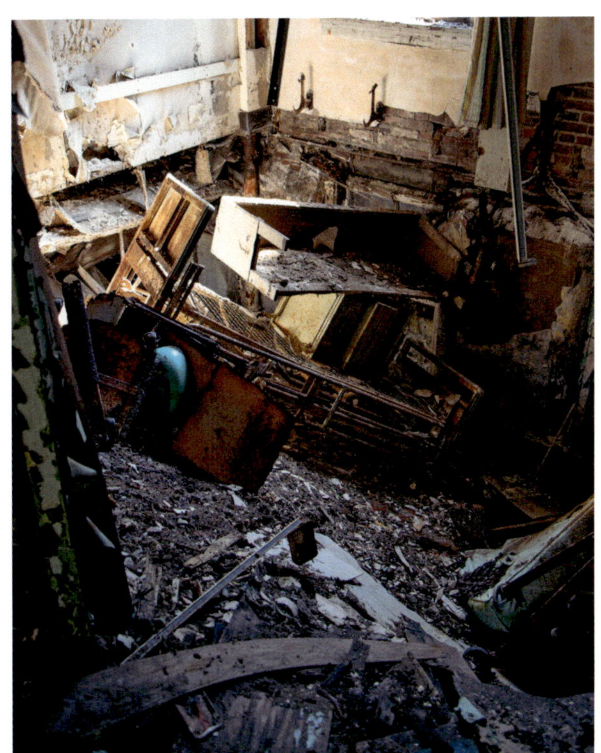

The hospital was dangerous, especially the patients rooms. Many had fallen into the basement and first floor.

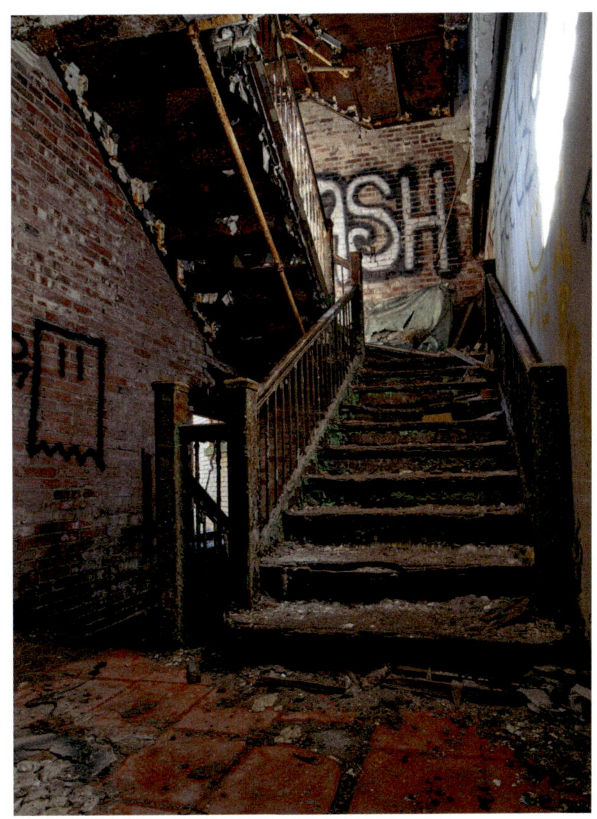

The main staircase to the hospital was rotting away. You could see through the steps where chunks of metal were missing.

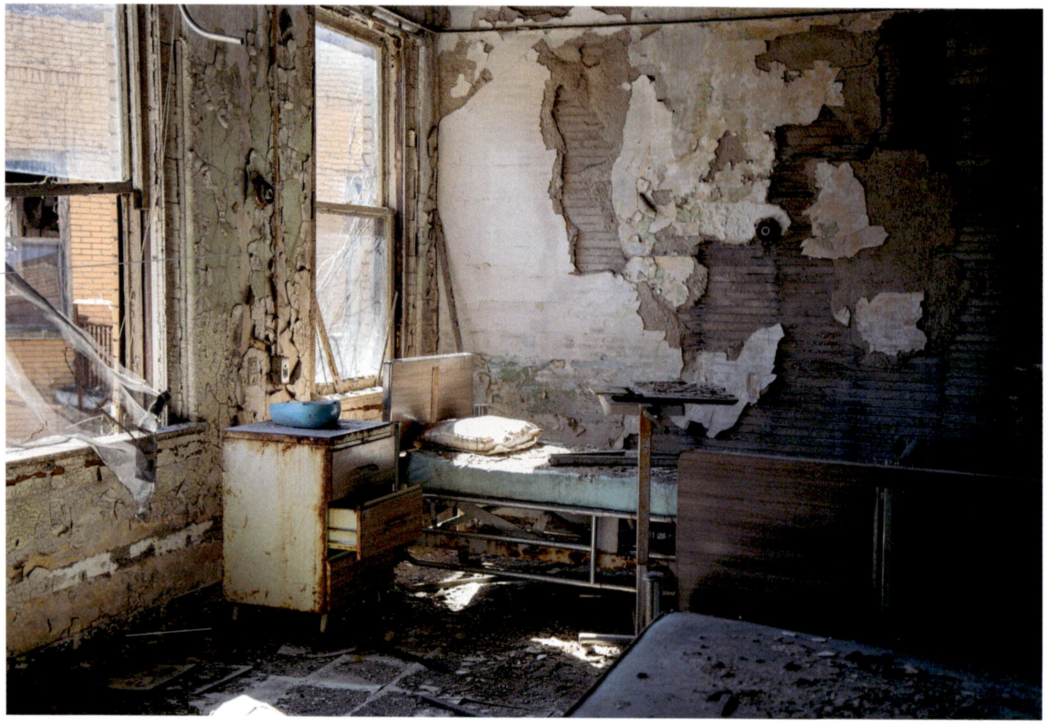

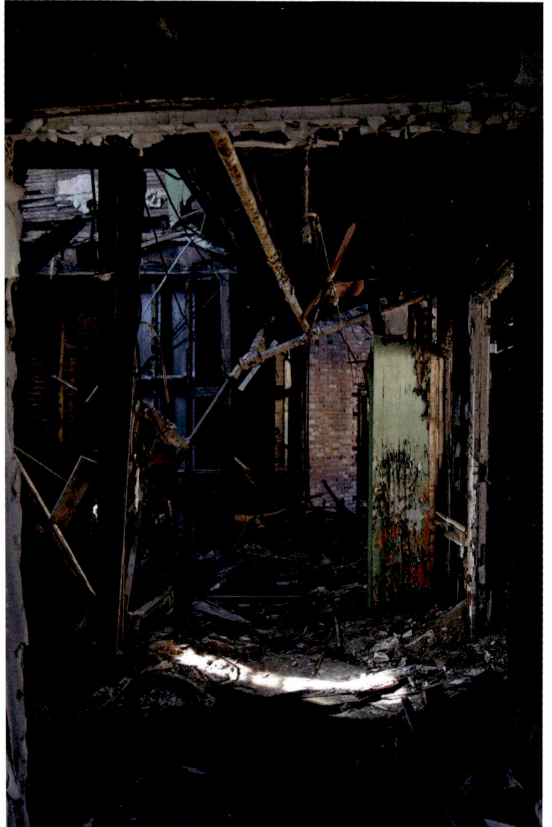

Above: Pillows, bedpans, and eating tables still filled the patient rooms.

Left: In this hospital wing, much of the second floor had collapsed, sending the first-level foundation into the basement.

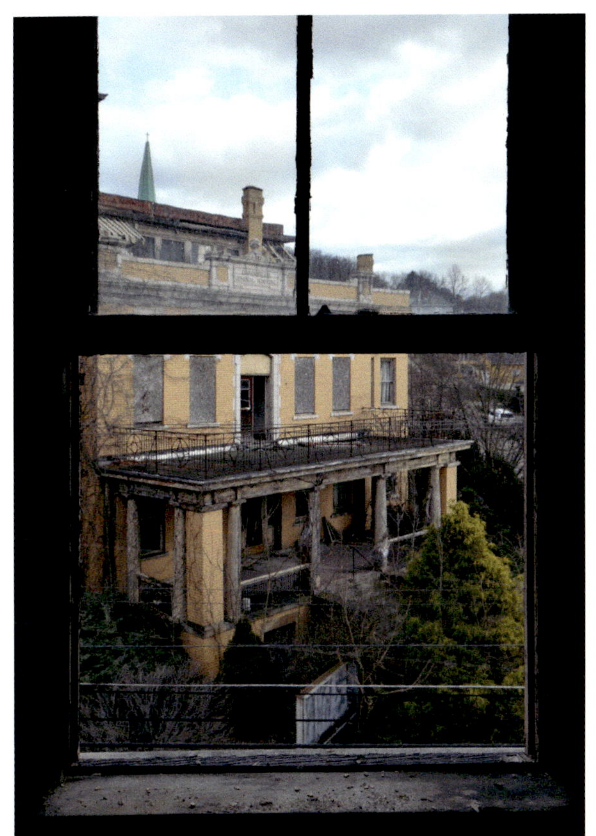

Right: View of the main hospital across the street from the Horner Nurse Home.

Below: Taken in February 2021, as demolition was in its final days.

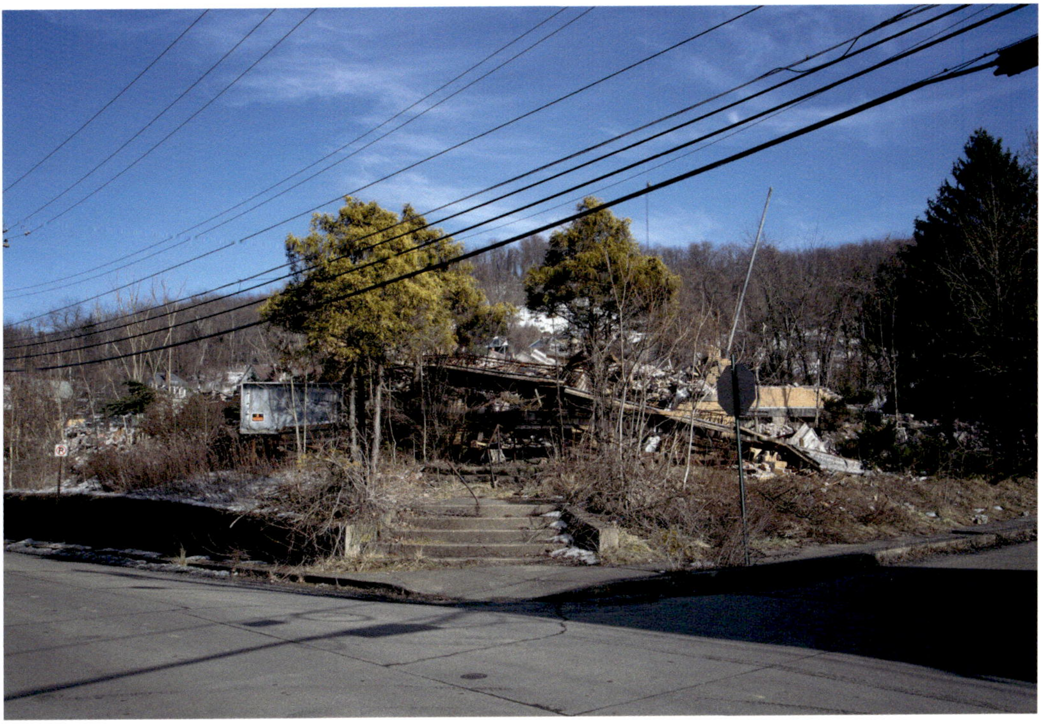

2

CARRIE BLAST FURNACES

On the north side of the Monongahela River near the Rankin Bridge sits two thirteen-story furnaces. Standing over 92 feet tall, the furnaces have a history of producing steel that was used to build the Sears Tower, the Empire State Building, the Golden Gate Bridge, the Gateway Arch, the George Washington Bridge, the Alaska oil pipeline, and the battleship USS Missouri. Built in 1884, the furnaces produced over 1,000 tons of iron daily. The property contains two furnaces, an ore yard, a car dumper, a torpedo car, a brick blower house, hot stoves, an engine-blowing house, a cast house, and a 15-ton crane. For every ton of iron produced, it took 4 tons of iron ore, coke, and limestone. They remained in operation until 1978. In 2006, they were elected a National Historic Landmark. They are some of the only pre-World War II twentieth-century blast furnaces that are still standing. Today, you can visit the furnaces through a non-profit organization that offers tours and other programs.

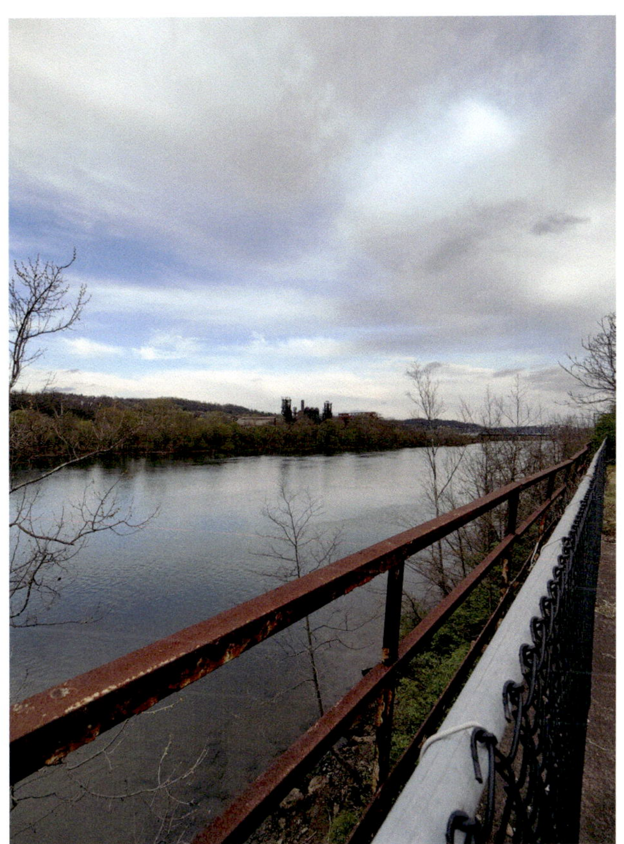

Right: The blast furnace is so grand it can be seen from across the Monongahela River.

Below: The furnaces get their name, Carrie, from the original owners.

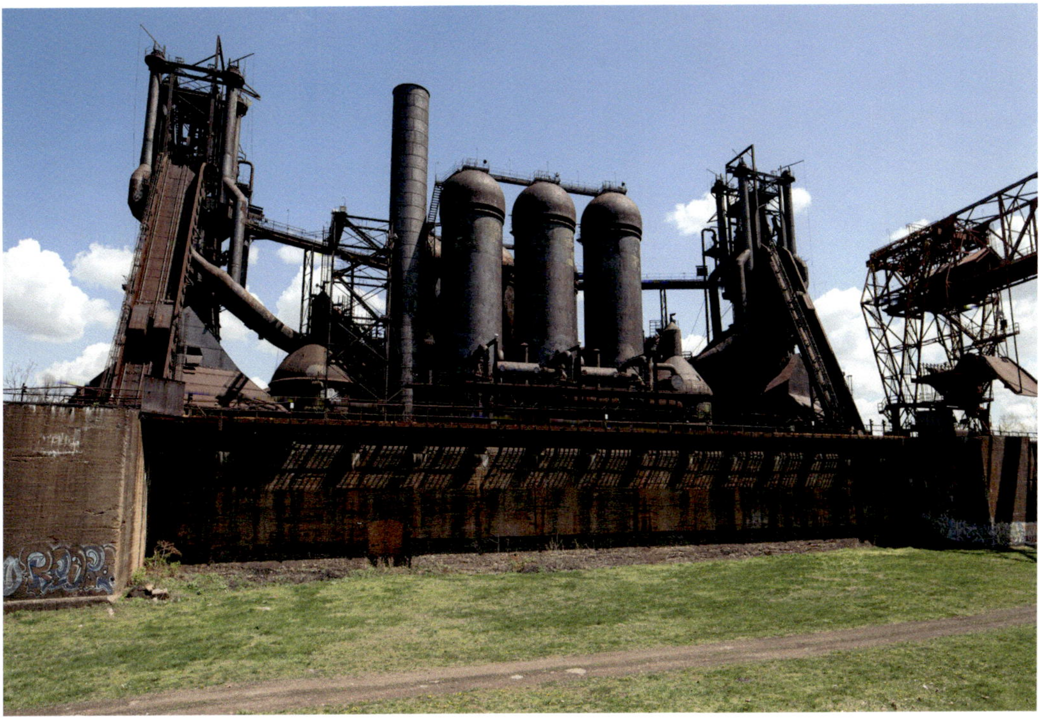

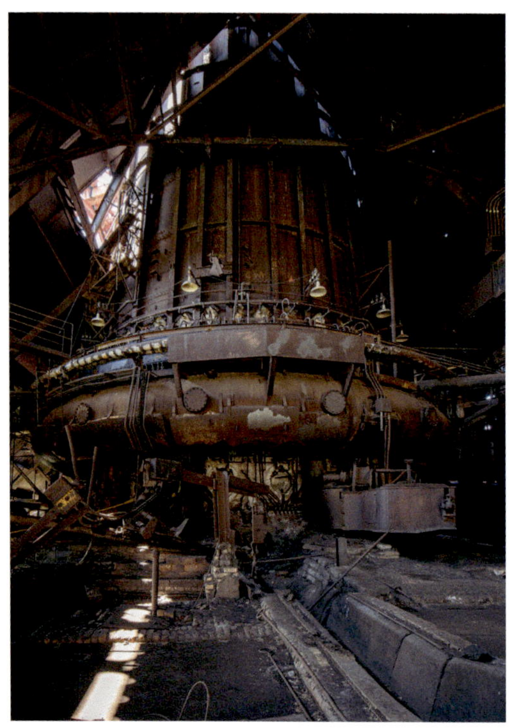

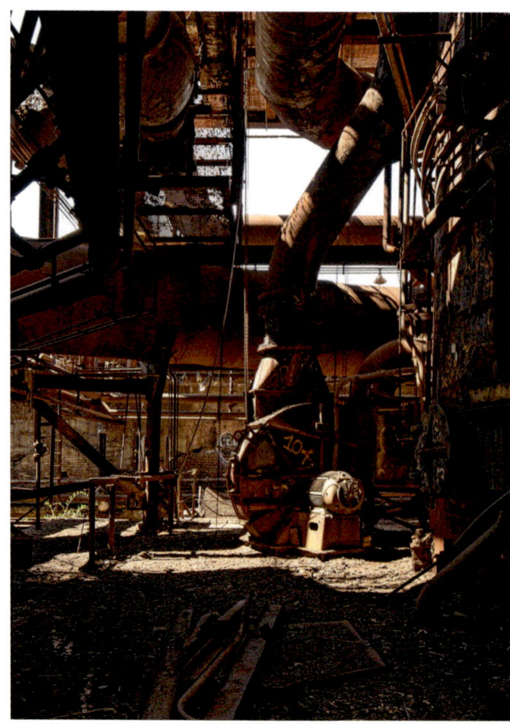

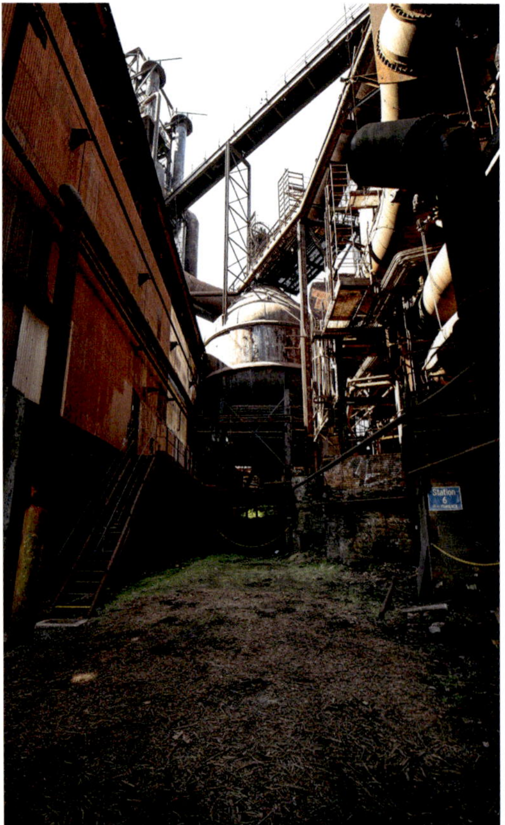

Above left: One of the massive blast furnaces.

Above right: Many of the pathways circle around the machinery.

Left: The cooling system for the furnaces utilized more than 5 million gallons of water a day.

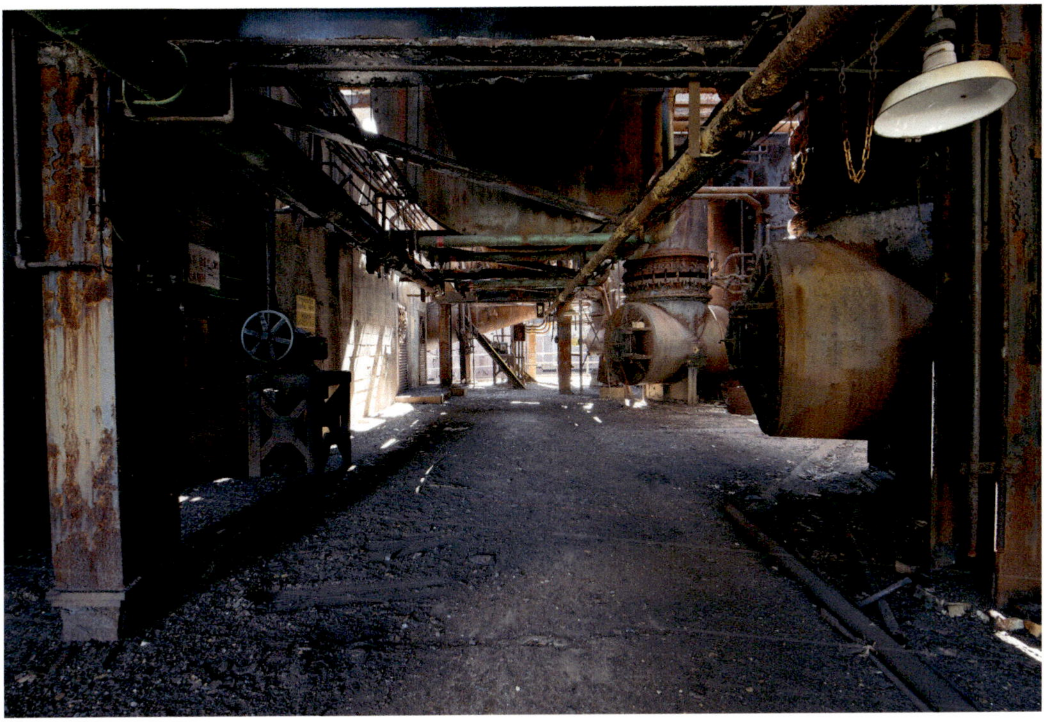

Above: A maze of pipes.

Right: Debris gathers under a decommissioned light fixture.

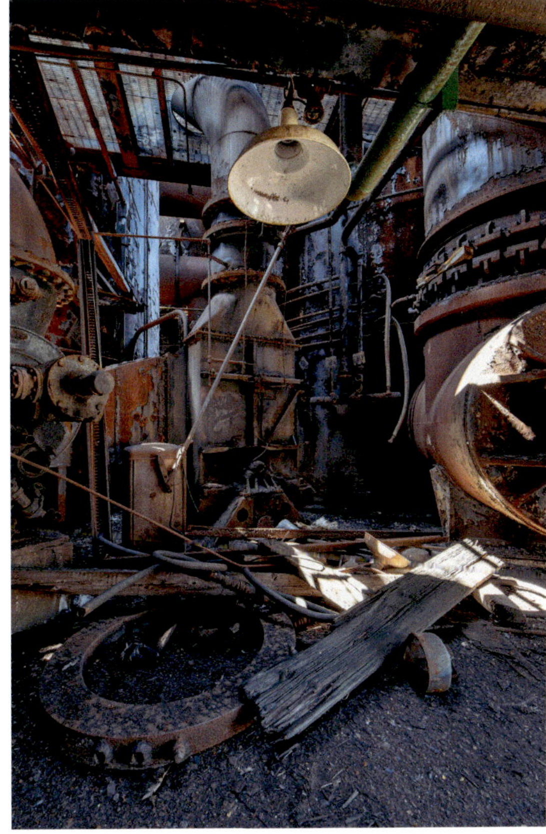

3

HILLCREST HOTEL AND LOUNGE

The Hillcrest Hotel and Lounge is located in Claysburg, Pennsylvania. The hotel, in addition to the lounge, had a bar and restaurant called the Country Apple. The building was originally an Econo Lodge. The sign shows a silhouette of the old name behind the new letters. There are thirty-two guest rooms in the hotel that once offered cable TV and a deluxe continental breakfast. I was unable to find a lot of history of the hotel. What I did find was that the property changed hands three times in the last twenty-one years. The most recent Google review was eight years ago, reporting the location closed.

I was amazed to find brochures in the main lobby, cans of food stocked in the kitchen, and the beds still made in the guest rooms. A recent visit to the area in 2022 showed signs of early demolition.

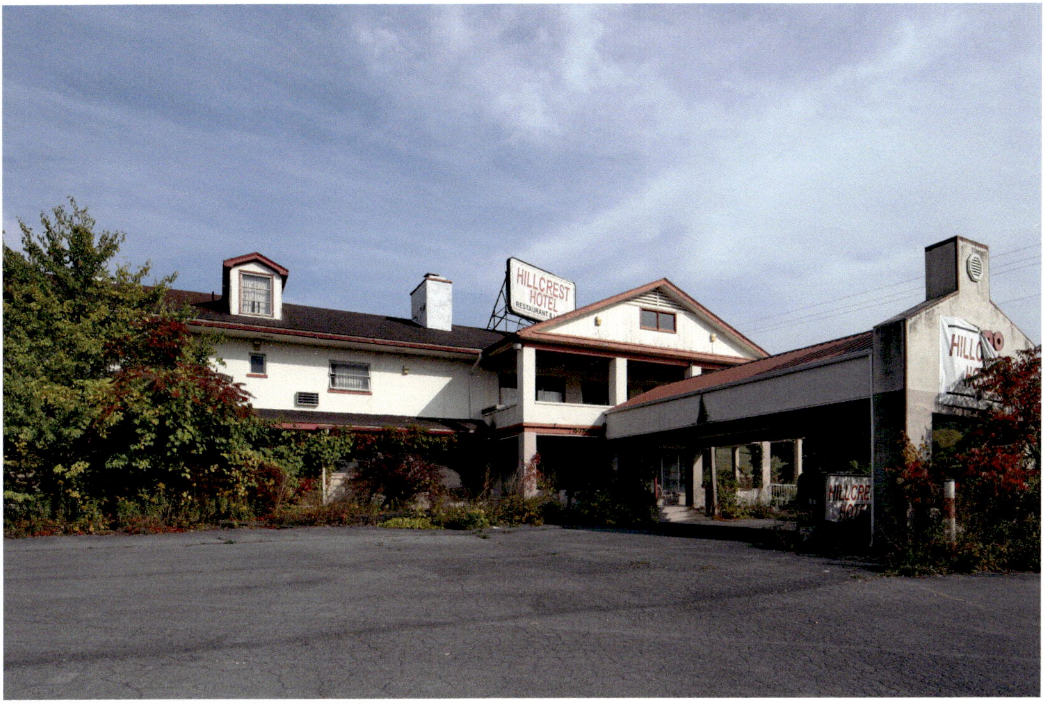

Above: The old Econo Lodge sign can be seen poking out from behind the Hillcrest Hotel banner.

Right: Brochures were still displayed in the hotel's main entryway.

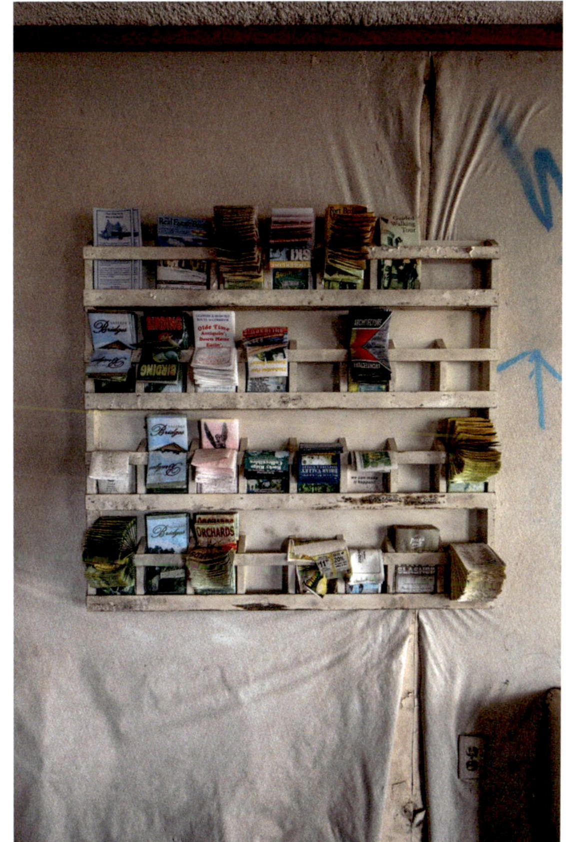

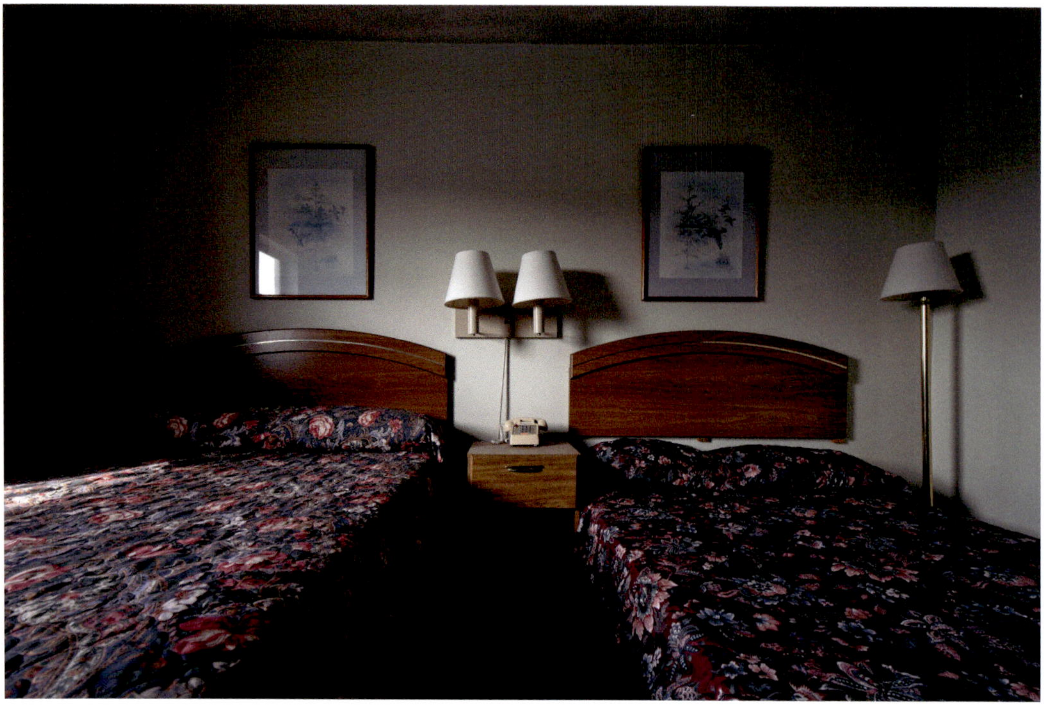

The hotel rooms are still made up and awaiting guests that will never come. The bedframes are beginning to collapse under the weight of the mattresses as the wood has weakened from the elements.

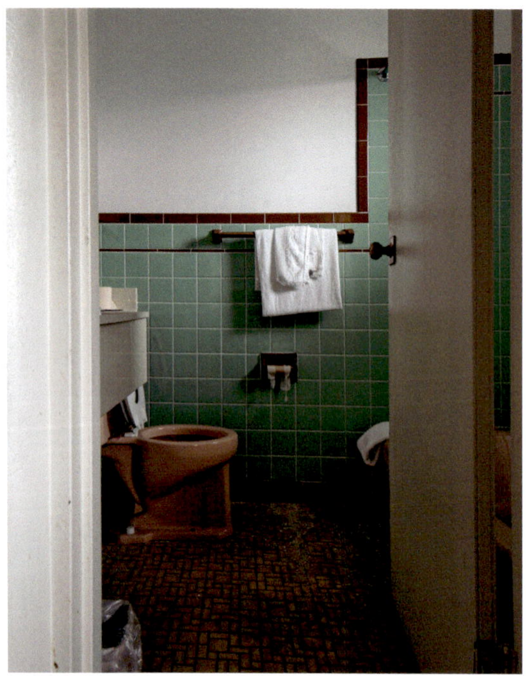

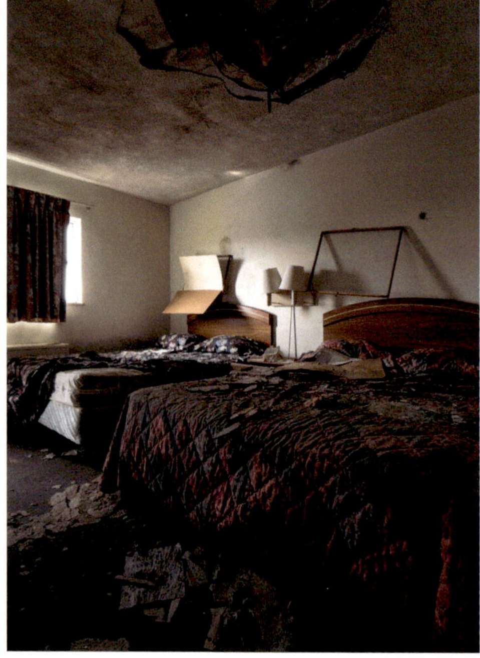

Above left: The bathrooms in the hotel were still stocked with linen and ready for guests to check-in.

Above right: Some of the rooms suffered a heavy amount of decay.

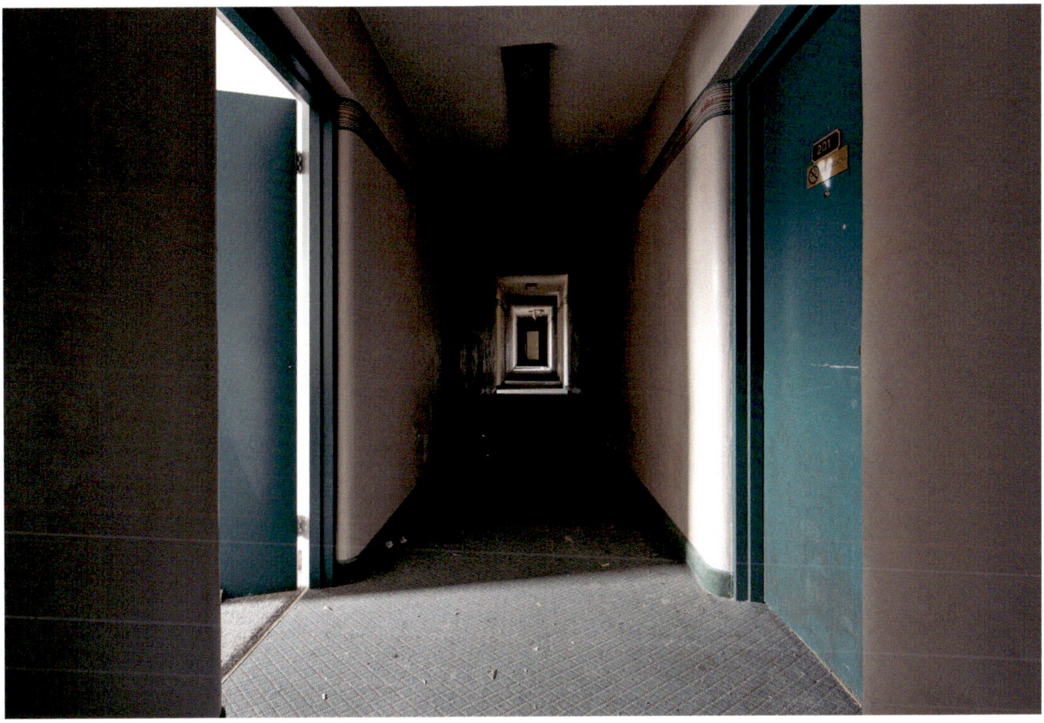

The disconnected electronic key system keeps many doors locked without entry.

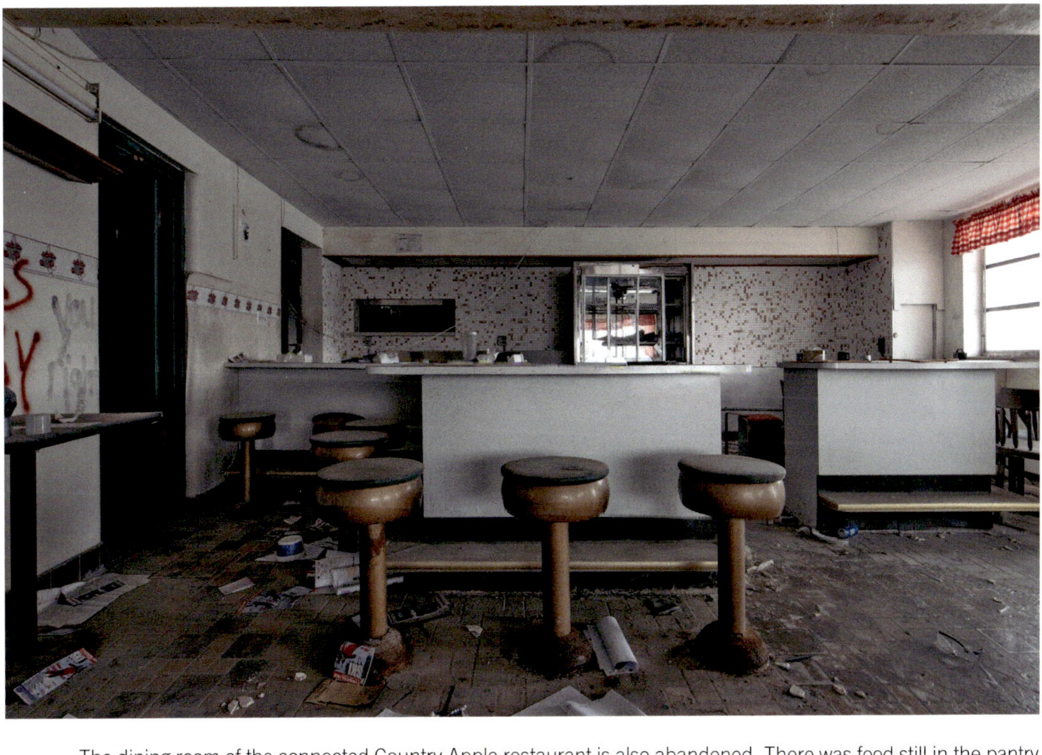

The dining room of the connected Country Apple restaurant is also abandoned. There was food still in the pantry and dishes in the kitchen.

4

HORNER MEMORIAL NURSES HOME

Built directly across from the Brownsville General Hospital, the nurses' home was named Horner Memorial Nurses Home after Joseph H. Horner. Construction was completed in 1929. The three-story building was made out of buff brick and Indiana limestone. The building contained a parlor, gymnasium, libraries, more than sixty sleeping rooms, a lecture room, a sewing room, a trunk room, a boiler room, and a kitchen. The roof of the building had a sunroof that overlooked Brownsville. The construction of the building cost around $130,000.

The school of nursing closed its doors for good in 1952. The Horner Memorial Nurses Home building became part of the Golden Age Nursing Home after the Brownsville General Hospital relocated. The nurses' home, which had sat empty for over twenty years, met the same fate as the hospital only a few months after.

Horner Memorial was a unique building to explore. Unlike the hospital, this building did not have hospital beds but rather wooden beds and desks in most of the rooms. The basement was completely flooded, so I could not explore the trunk room, lecture room, gymnasium, and sewing room that were rumored to have been located down there. There appeared to be a two-level type of basement. I was able to find the kitchen and a sitting room with a piano. The rest was down a flight of stairs that was submerged in water. The view from the roof of the nurses' home was quite beautiful.

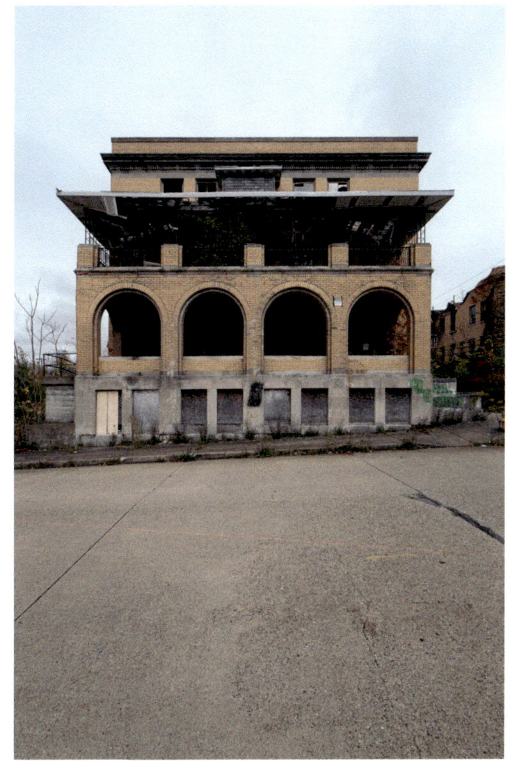

Right: A street view of the side of the Nurse Home.

Below: The front door of the building shows incredible character. Sadly, the stone depicting the name above the door was not saved.

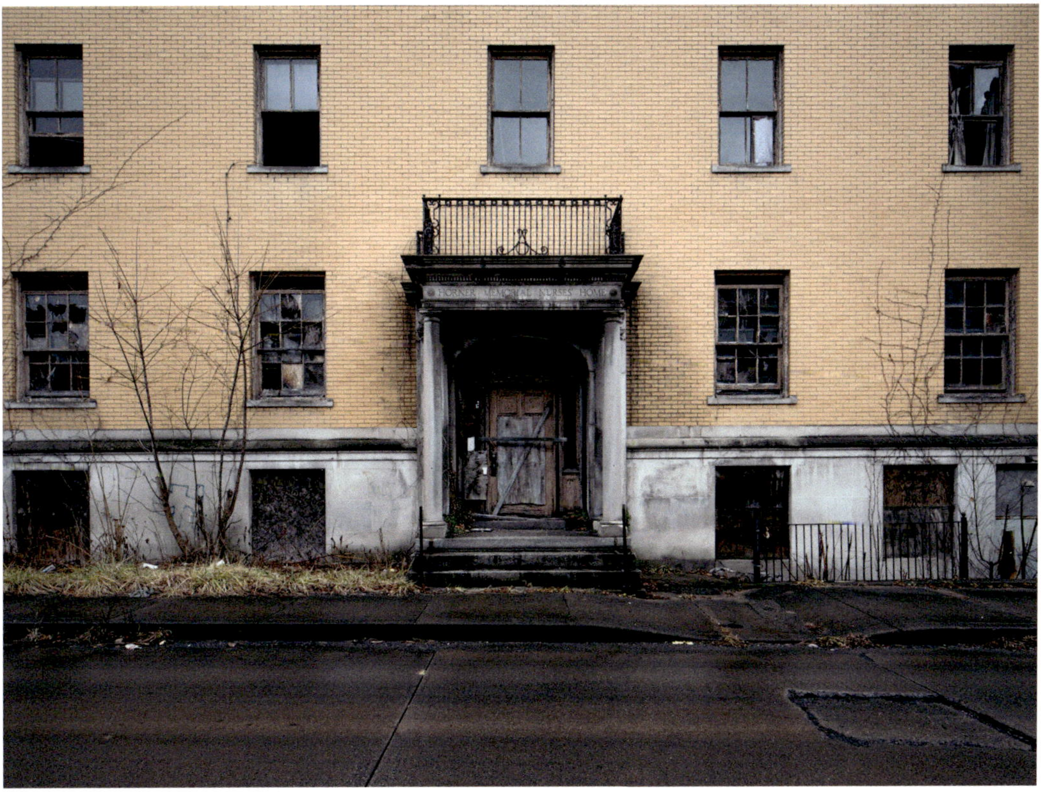

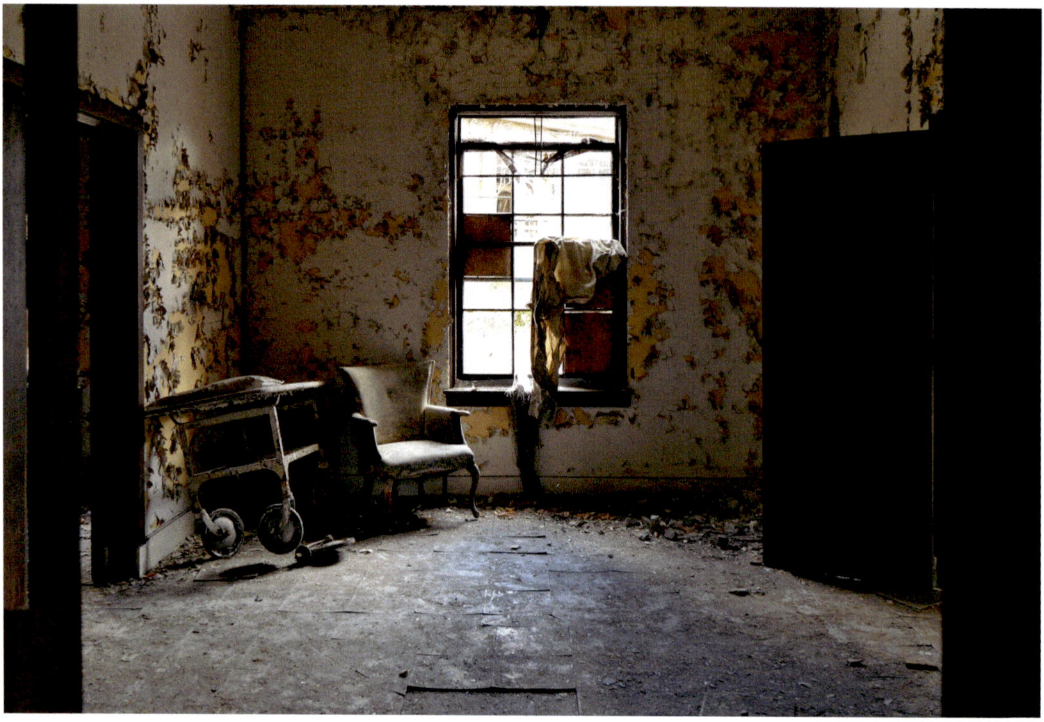

A gurney missing a wheel and chair sit in the corner.

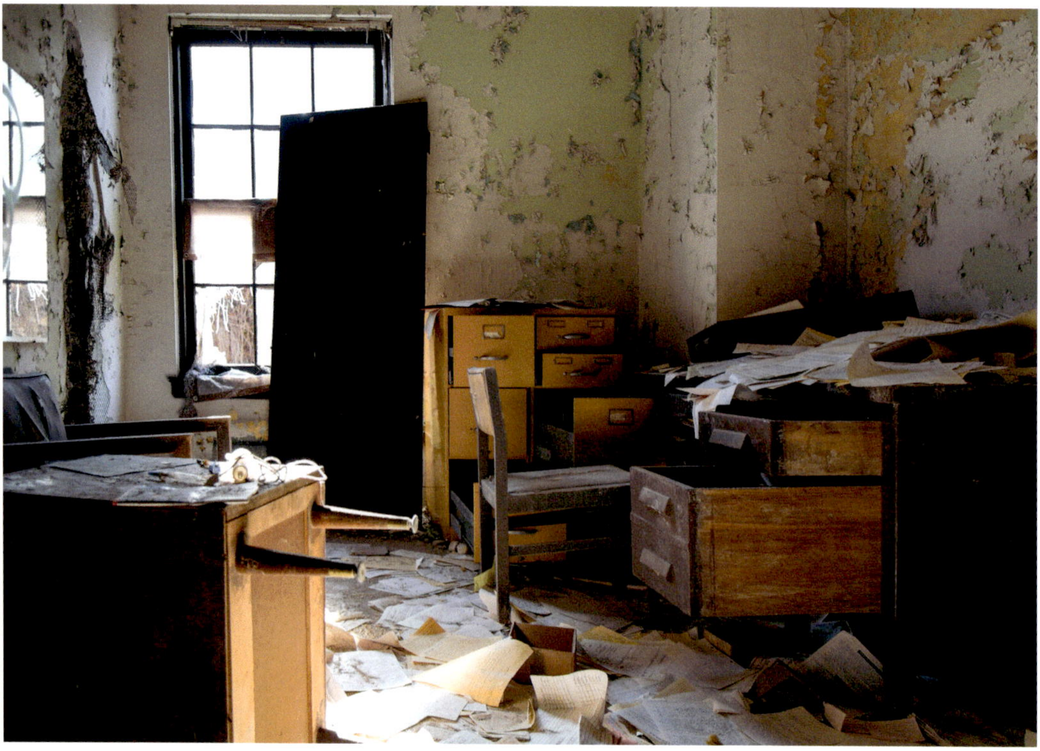

The main office of the building appeared to have been ransacked.

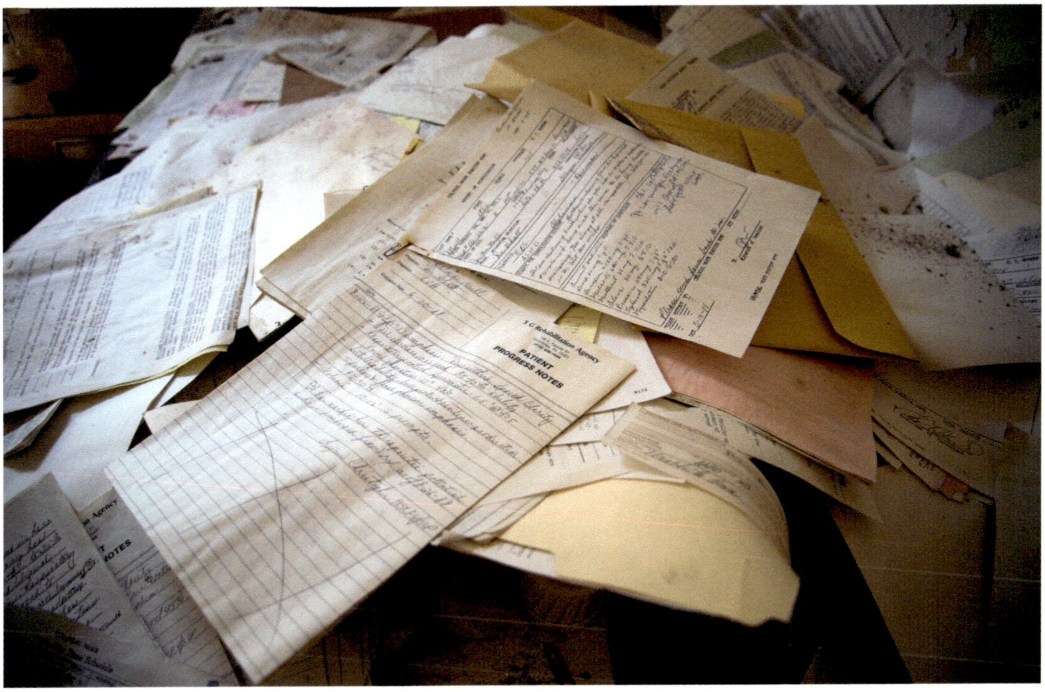

Medical records blanketed the desk in the main office.

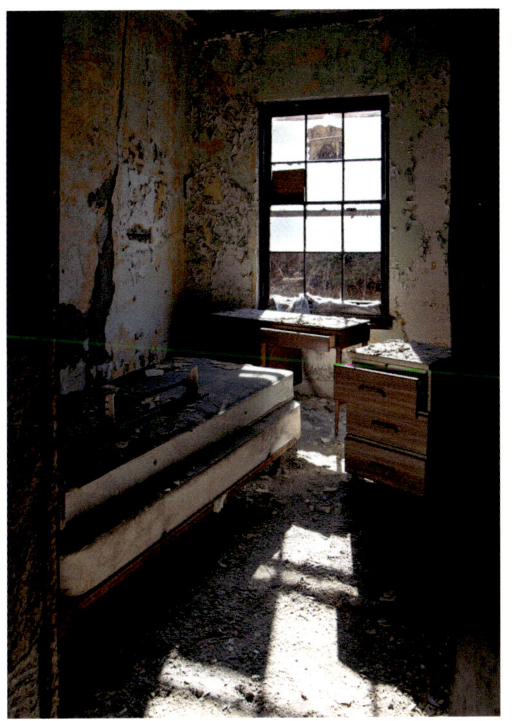

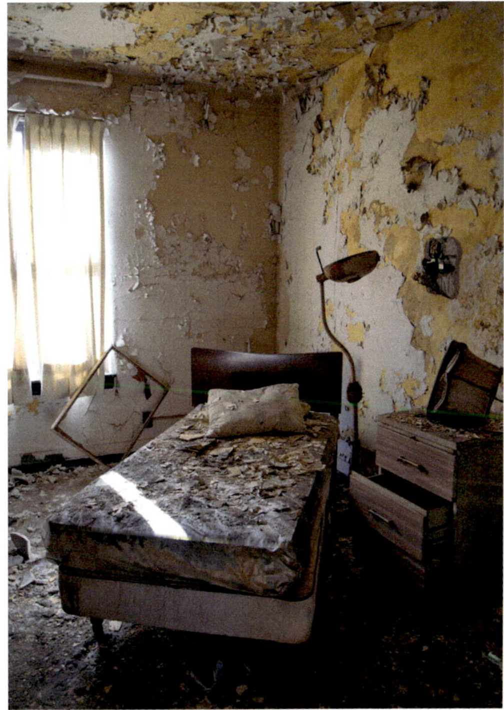

Above left: Just like the hospital, the rooms in the home were still furnished.

Above right: Where patients once laid, yellow paint chips have taken their place.

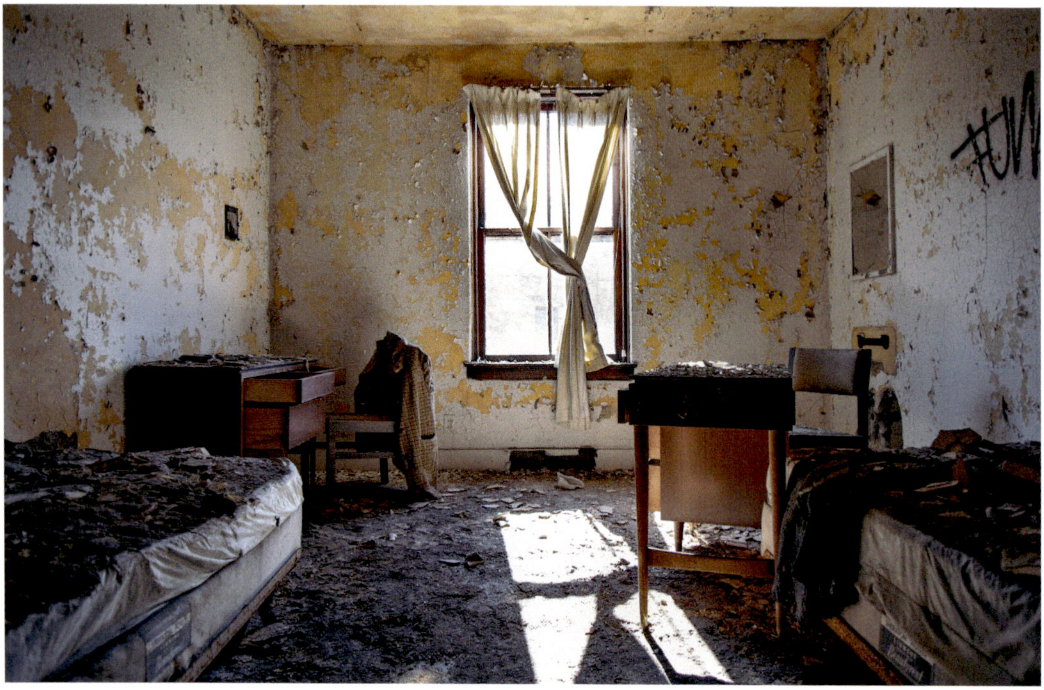

A jacket is left strewn on the back of a chair.

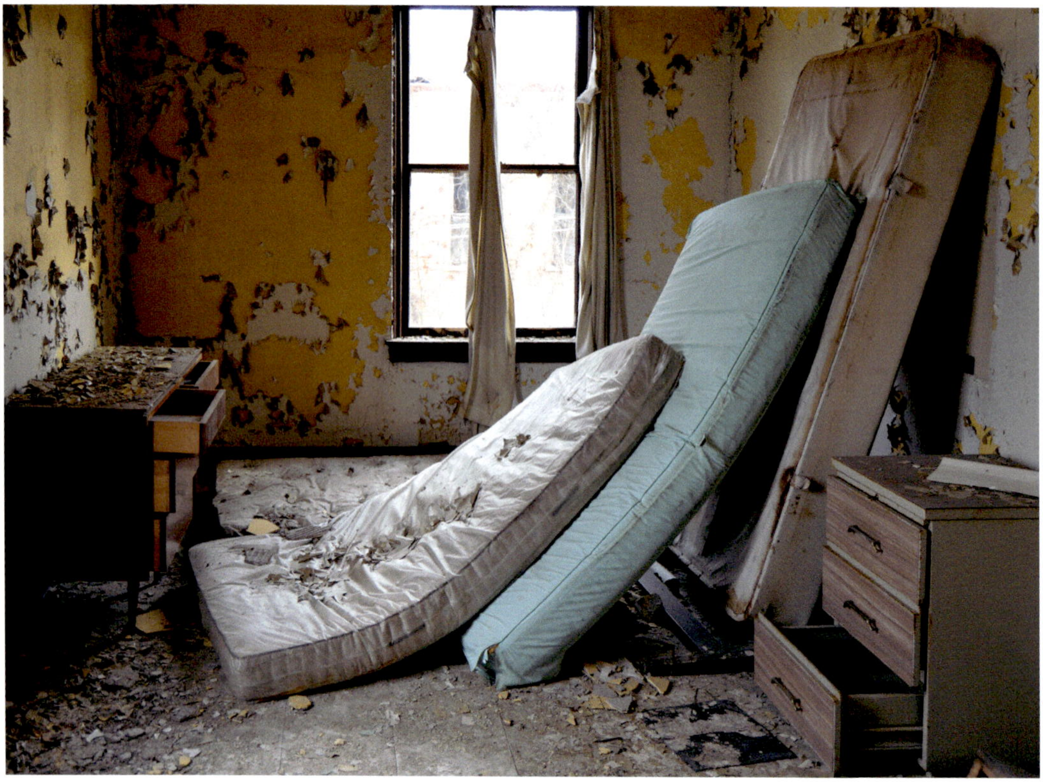

Mattresses stacked up in one of the rooms begin to collapse as time passes.

5

LADIES OF THE GRAND ARMY REPUBLIC HOME

The Ladies of Grand Army Republic Home was built in 1890, just under 10 miles from Pittsburgh. This twelve-room home was built for the Union Army veteran's indigent family members. The home burnt down in 1900. Replacing the original structure was a fifty-three-room facility that was eventually expanded in 1937, adding thirty more rooms. The front of the structure faced the railroad rather than the street. The home closed in 1996 and was purchased in 2001 with plans to repurpose the building. Those plans fell through, and the property was sold again in 2008. LGAR laid in ruins until it was eventually torn down in 2018.

This was one of my favorite-looking buildings in PA. It really was grand. It was unfortunate that it was exposed to the elements and left to fall into ruin. This vast building was slowly being taken over by vines and graffiti from vandals. As the back of the building faced the main room, many people drove past without even a glance in its direction.

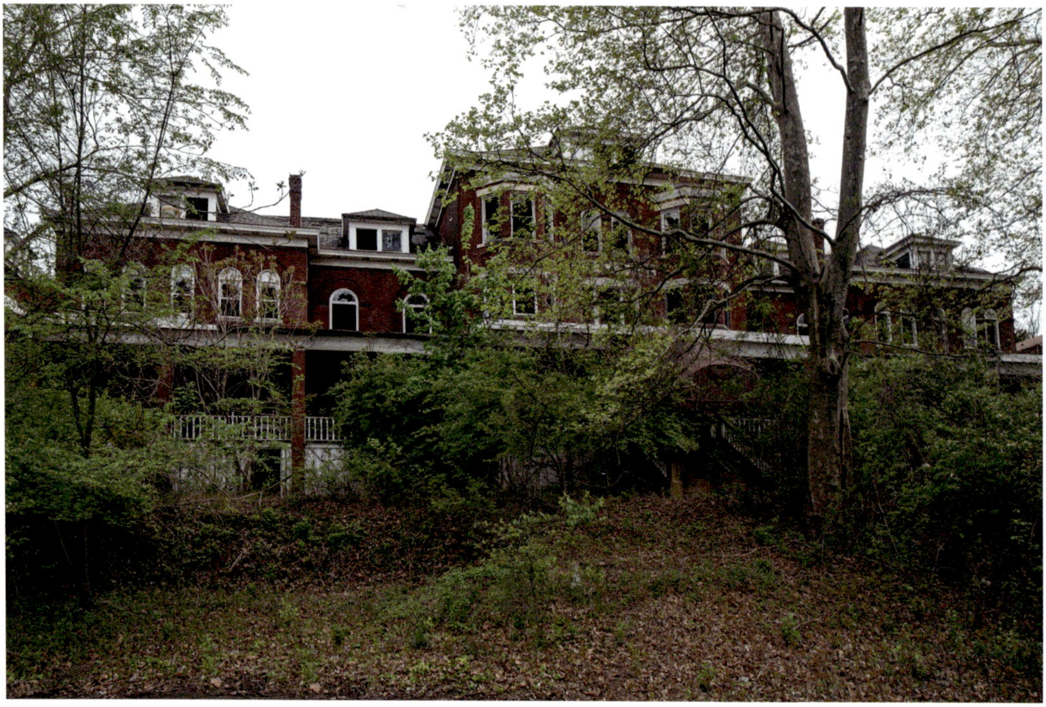

The front of the building faced the railroad tracks. The back of the building was all that could be seen from the road.

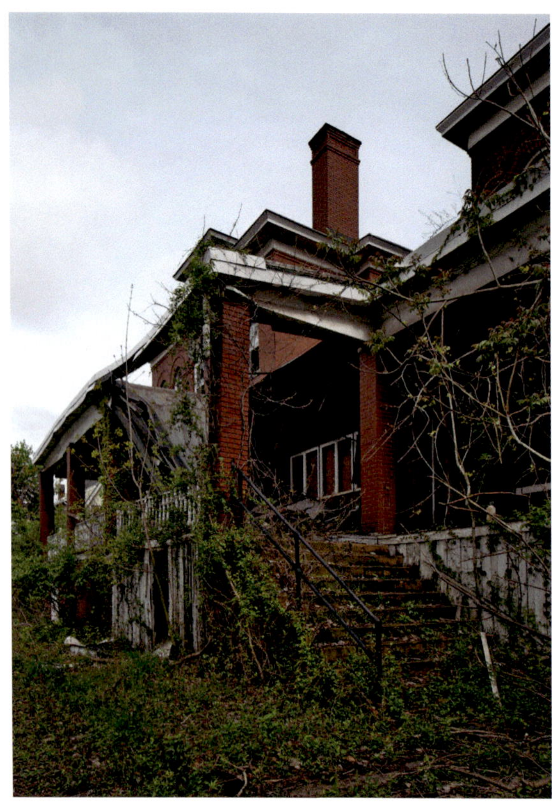

The porch's roof collapsed, and vines stormed the walls of the building.

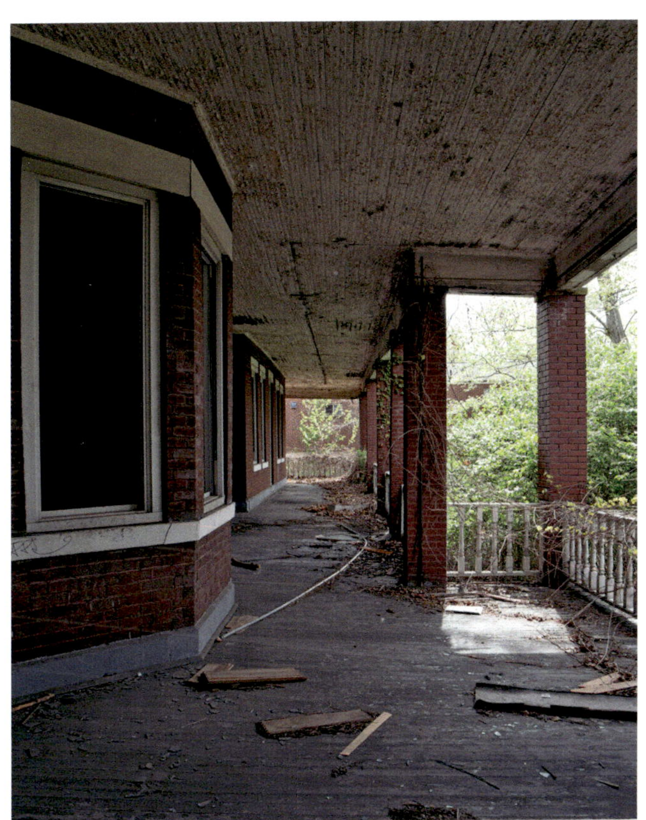

All of the windows were either broken or missing.

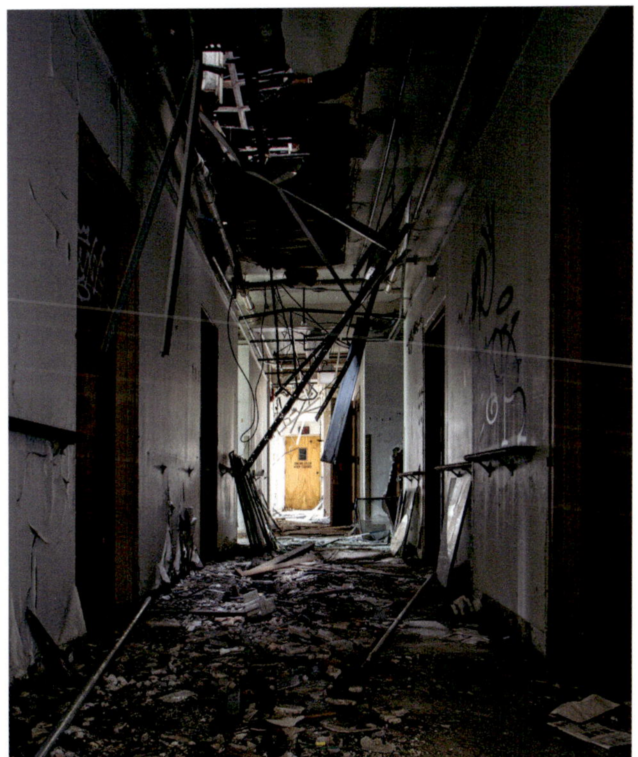

Water damage from holes in the roof caused the upper levels to collapse. You can see the floor above in this hallway.

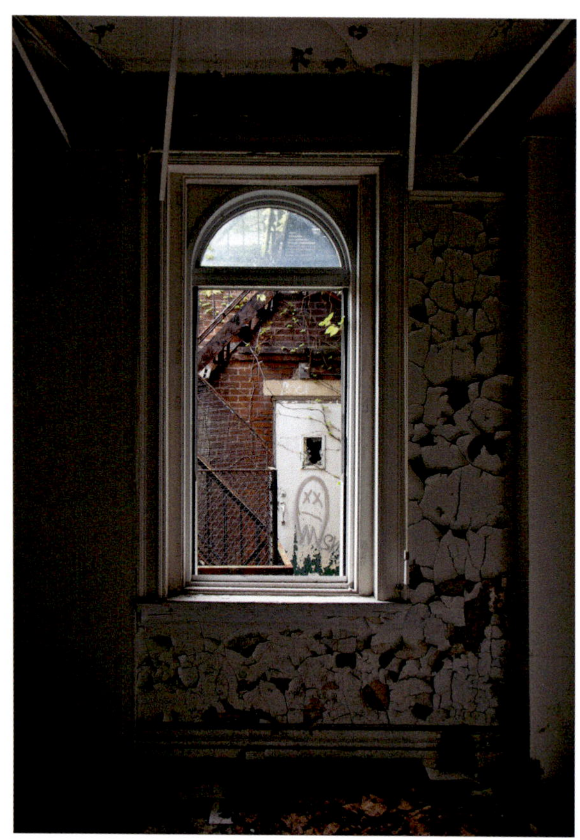

A rusted old fire escape can be seen from the window of one of the patient's rooms.

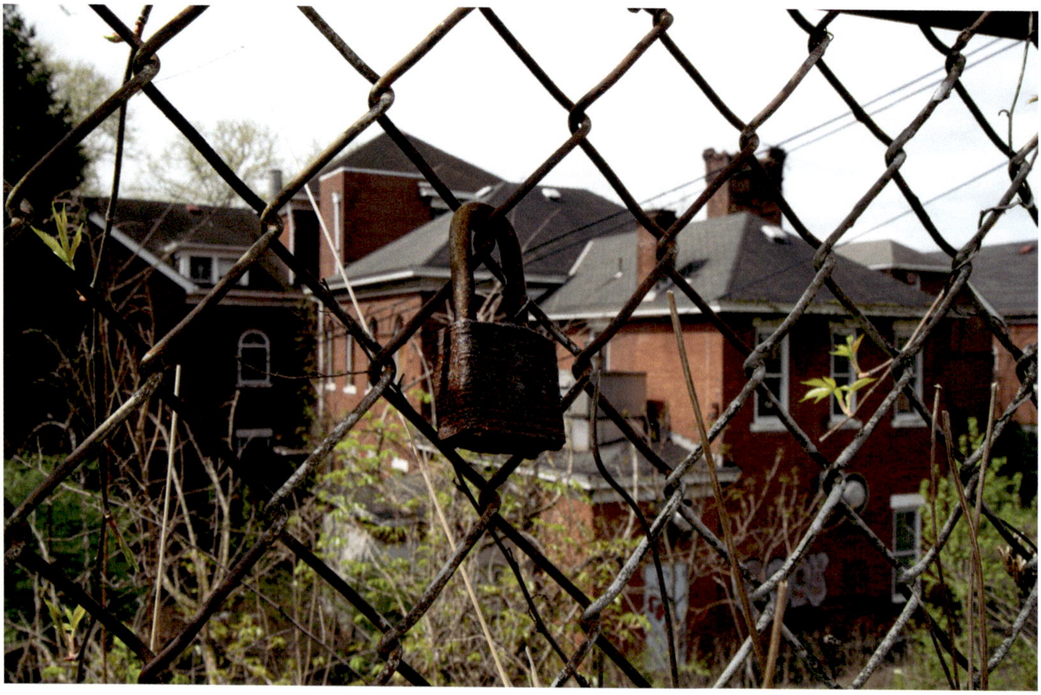

An old lock on the fence behind the building.

6

LINCOLN WAY

The mystery behind the 1.5-mile-long residential street in Clairton, Pennsylvania, remains unsolved. At least two dozen homes were located on Lincoln Way. It is not entirely clear why these families left everything behind. Between 1970 and 2009, the homes slowly, one by one, were left empty until the last house was abandoned in 2012. Walking down into this neighborhood on a very foggy Thanksgiving Day, I remember thinking to myself that I had never seen anything like it. While some of the homes were no longer standing due to arson, many were. Rummaging through the debris, old photos, teddy bears, and numerous personal belongings could be found left behind. Today, there is nothing left of the homes that once lined the street.

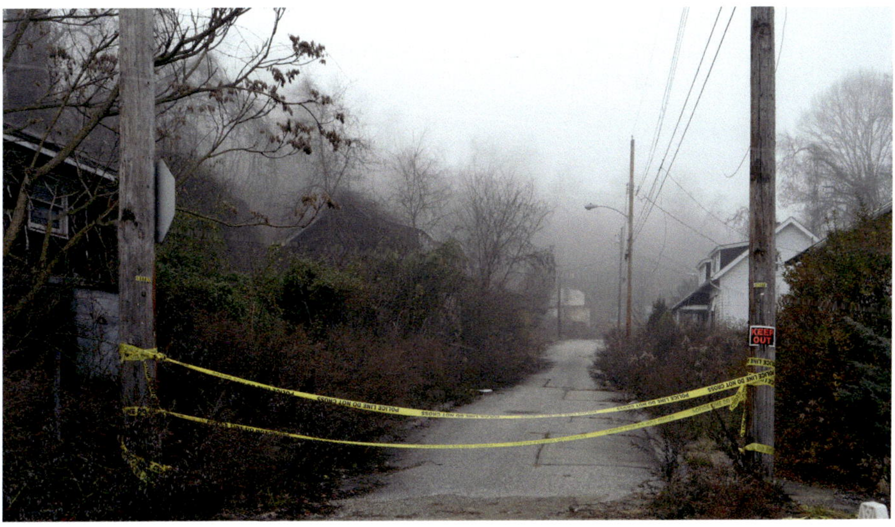

The road was blocked with caution tape and a sign that reads "KEEP OUT."

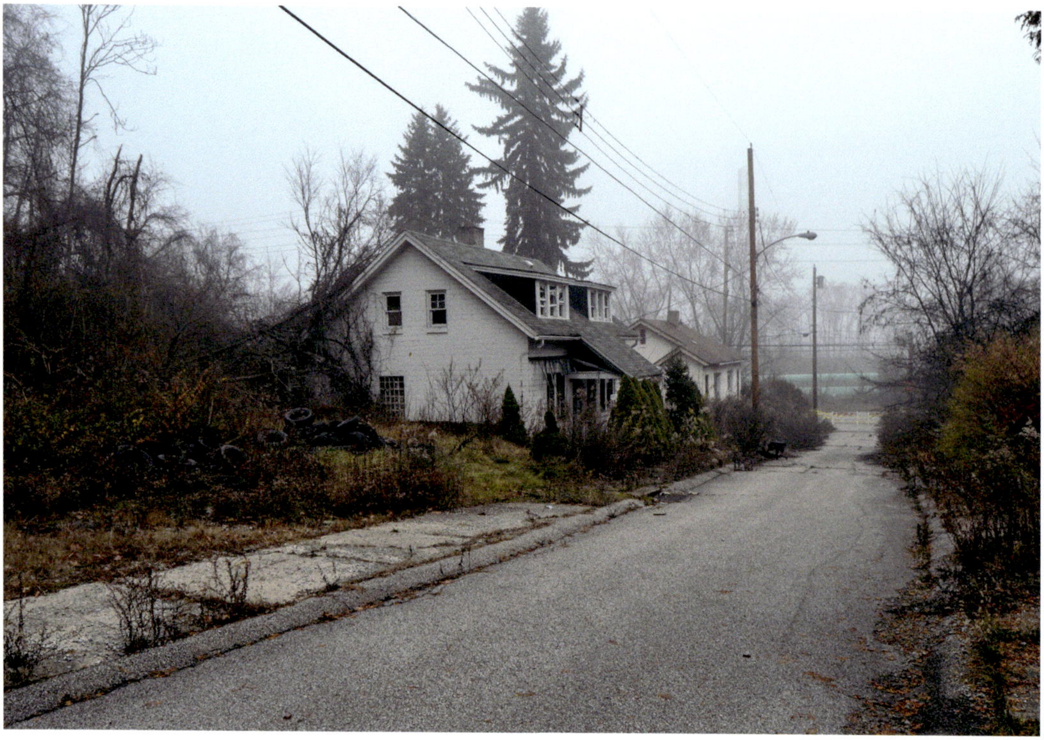

Many of the homes burnt down, but few remained.

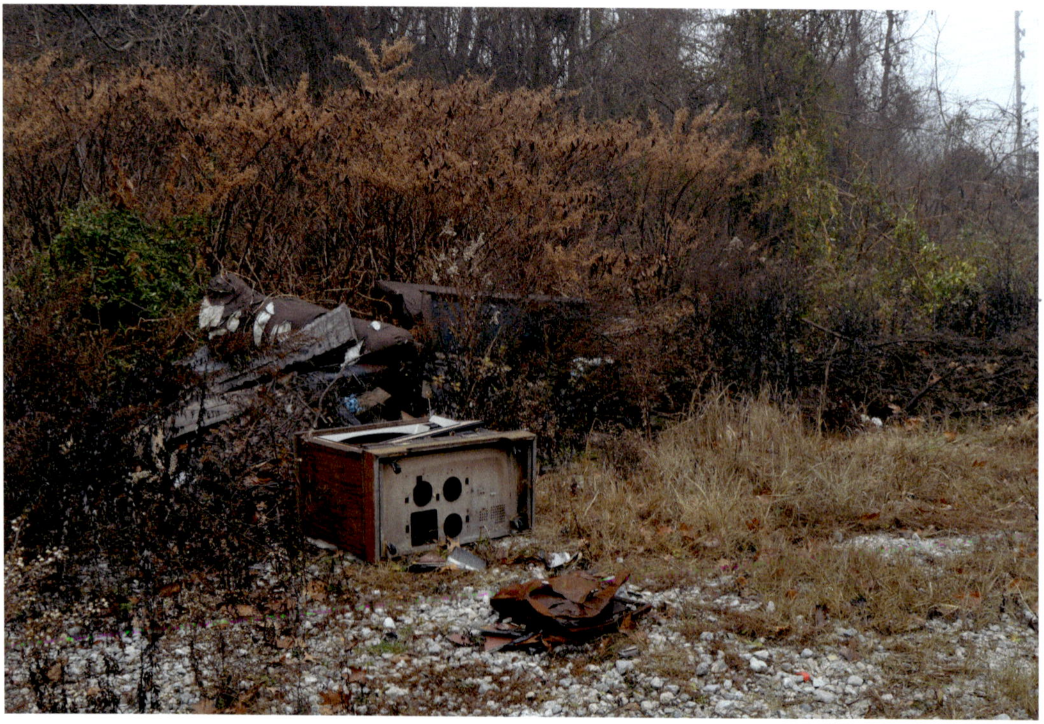

Couches and old TVs were removed from the vacant homes or dumped on the property.

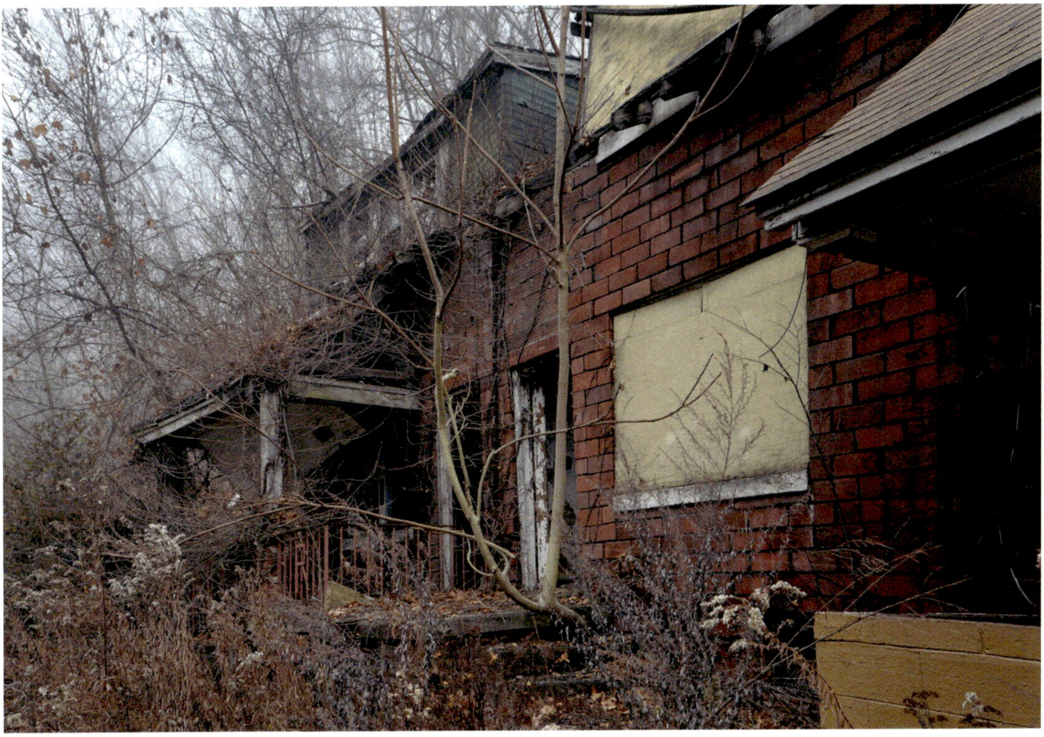

Trees were beginning to grow out of the steps leading to the homes.

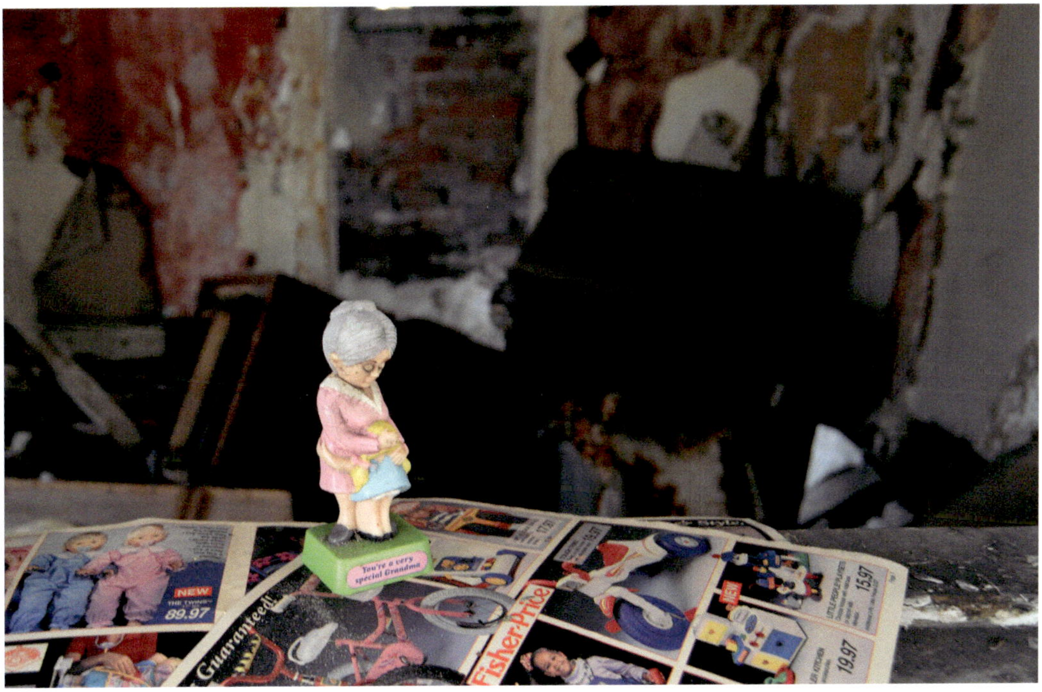

An old figurine is left on the windowsill of one of the homes. You can see much of it is collapsing into the basement.

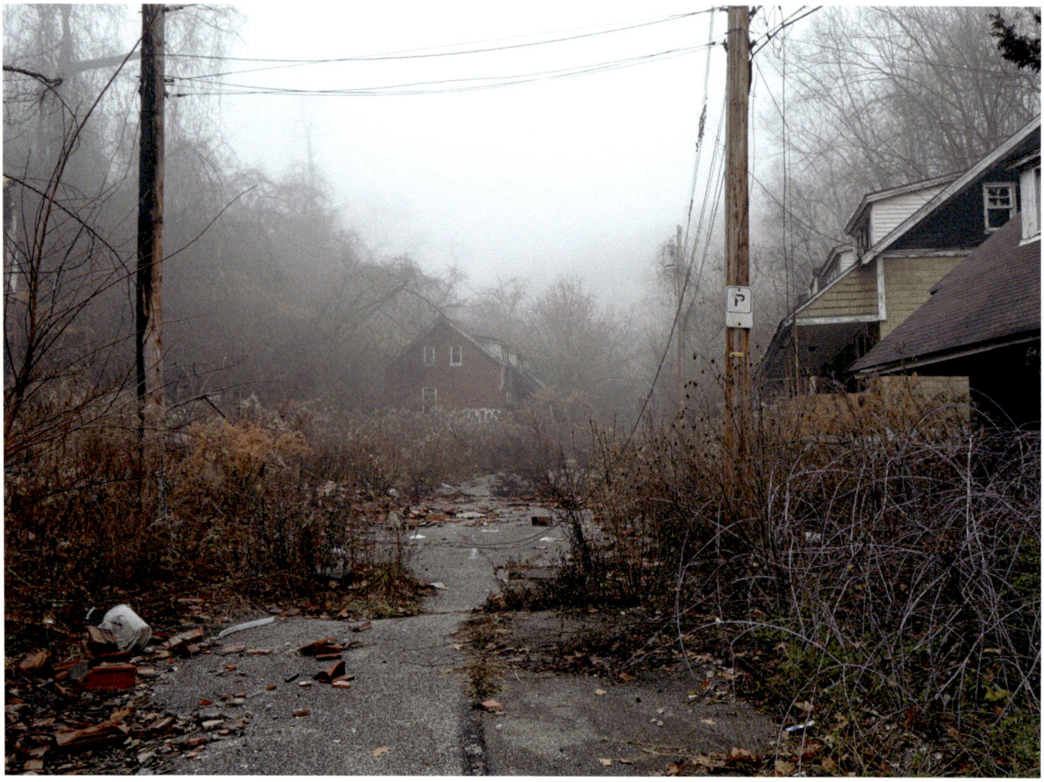

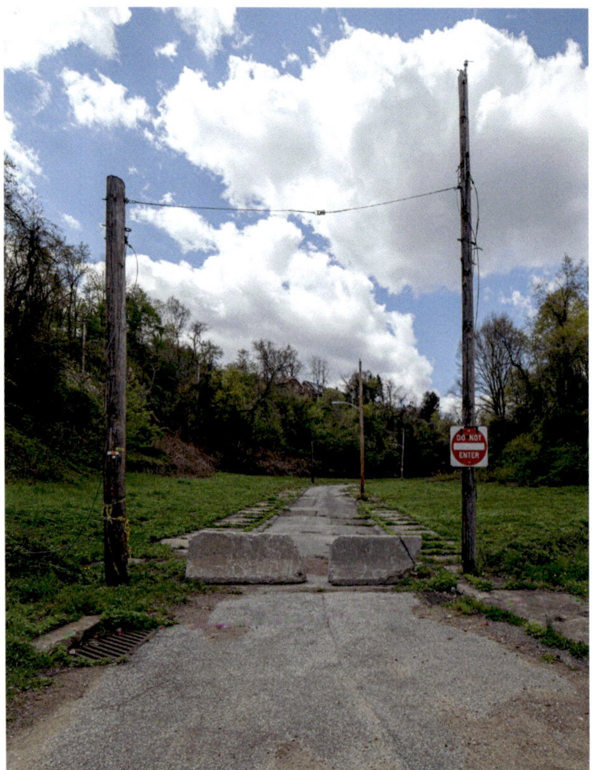

Above: There are more houses up around the bend.

Left: If you were to visit today, this is what you would find—an empty street with a strange past.

7

THE CITY OF McKEESPORT

In the 1900s, McKeesport was a center of steel manufacturing. In 1940, the city had a population of over 55,000. When steelmaking left the area, there was a decline in the economy. Today, the population is under 19,000, leaving much of the city abandoned. I often refer to this city as a mini-Gary after Gary, Indiana, which also fell victim to a decline in population, leaving much of the city vacant. McKeesport has many abandoned homes, churches, and businesses.

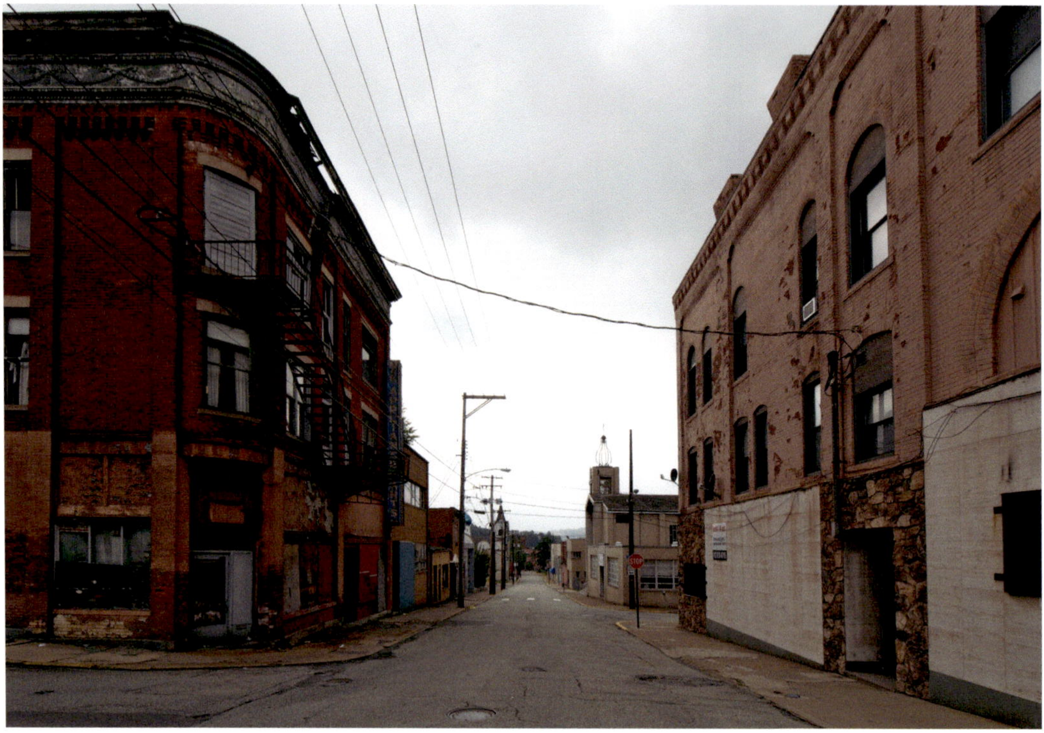

Many businesses remain empty on the main streets in this once-bustling town.

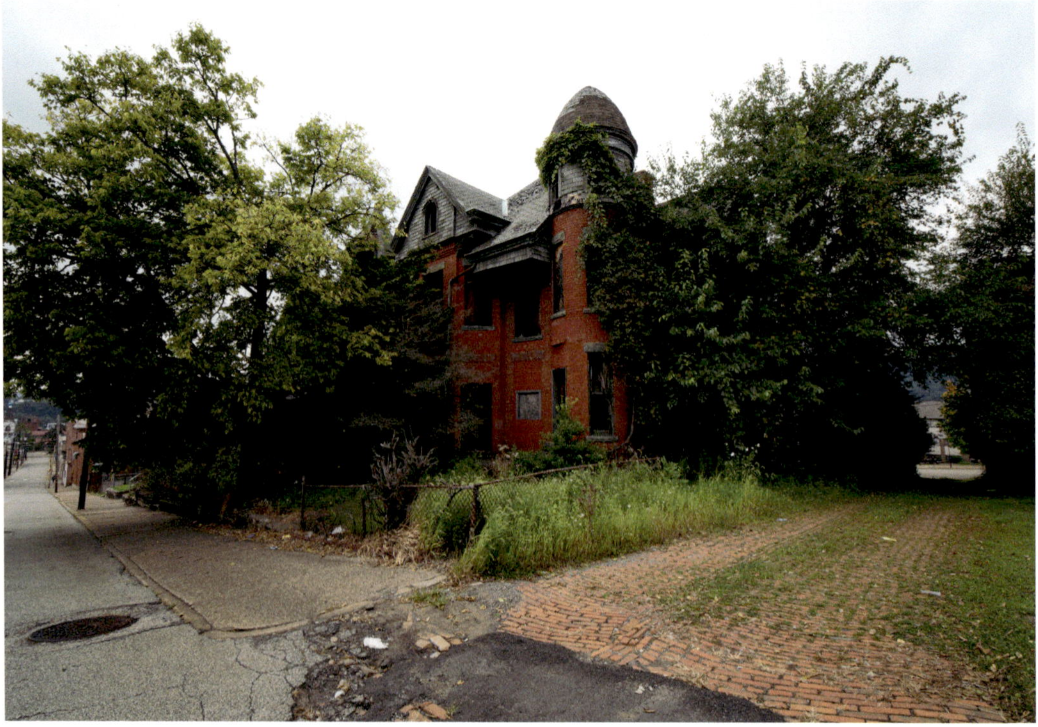

Two twin mansions sit side by side on a main street in the city.

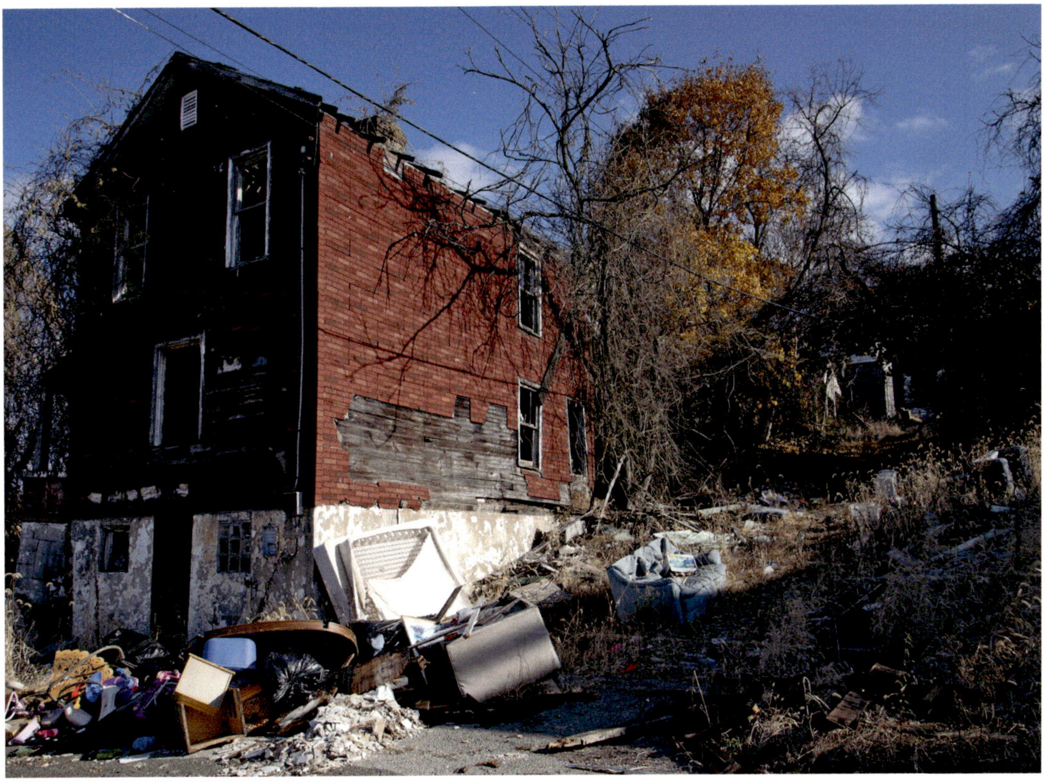

Above: Many abandoned homes have unfortunately become dumping grounds.

Right: A kiddie pool filled with dirty stagnant water in a living room surrounded by furniture and ceiling debris.

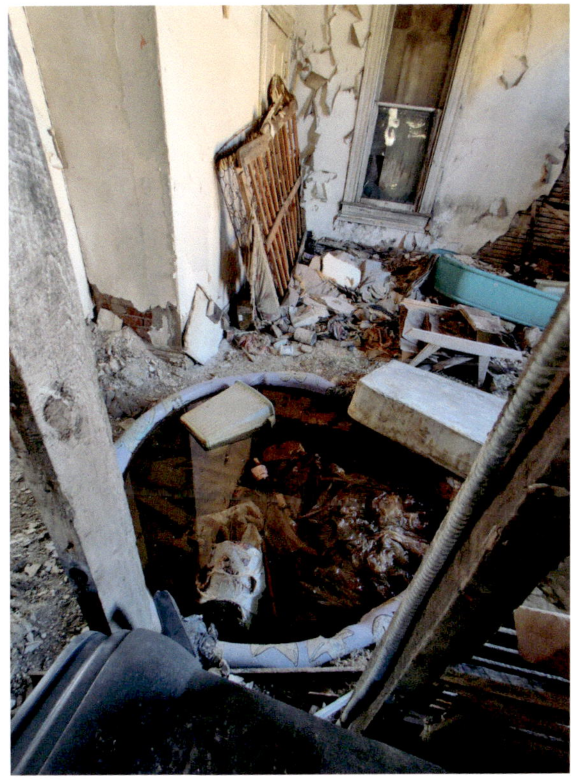

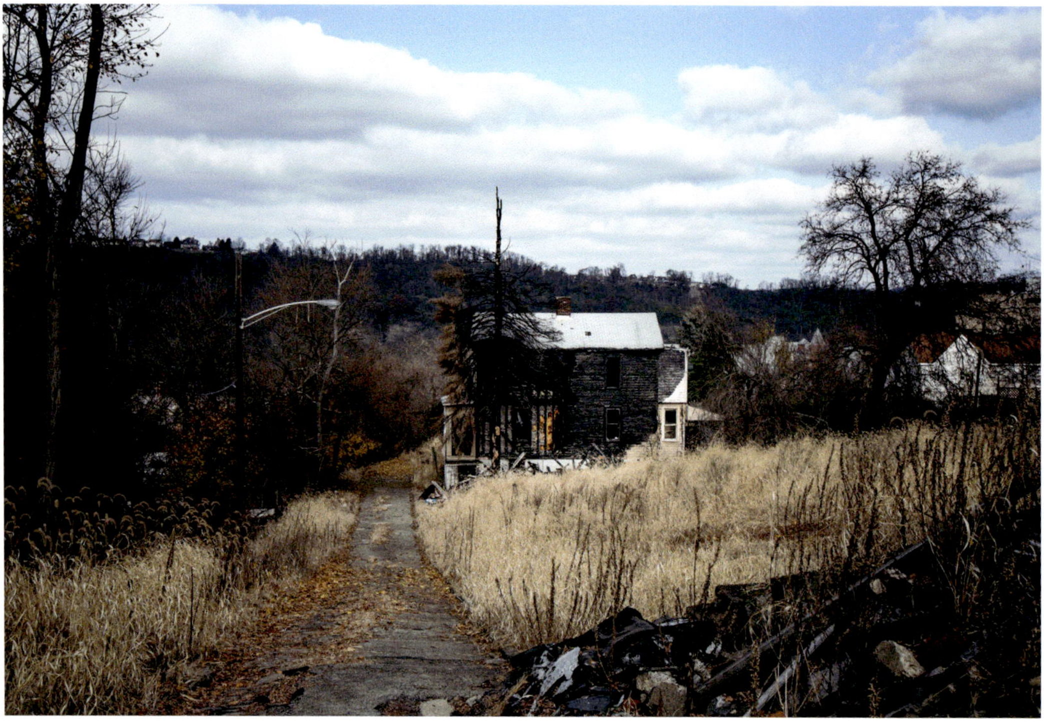

A charred tree still standing next to a house that caught fire. Trees and vines overtake this abandoned home.

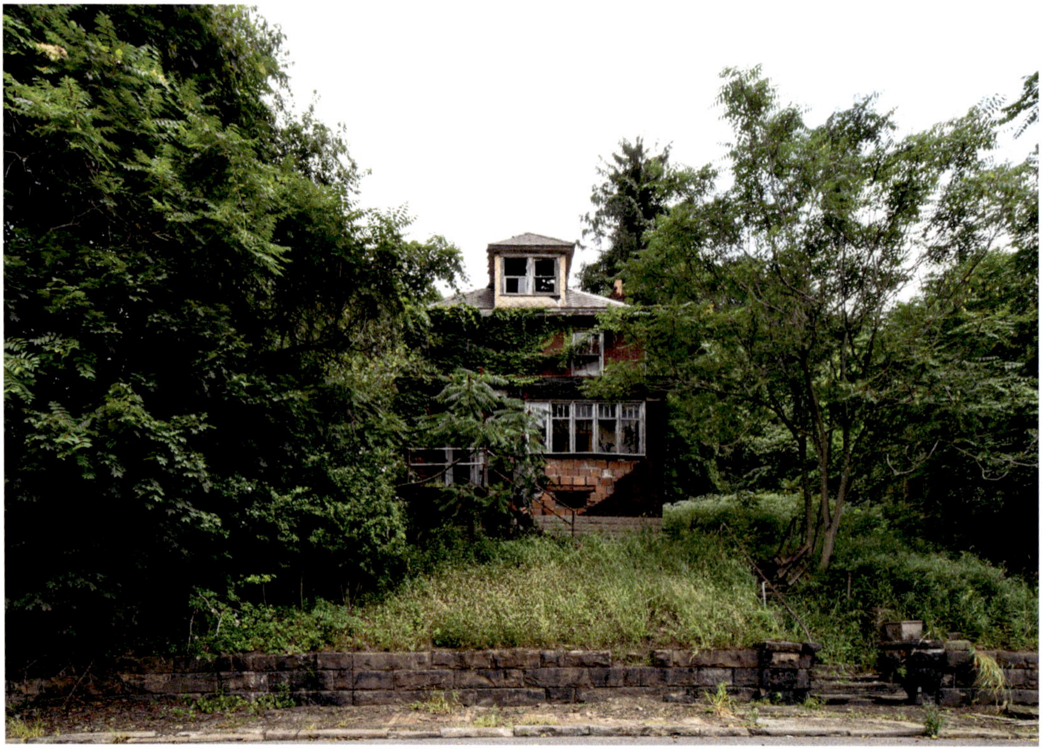

Trees and vines take over this unique brick house.

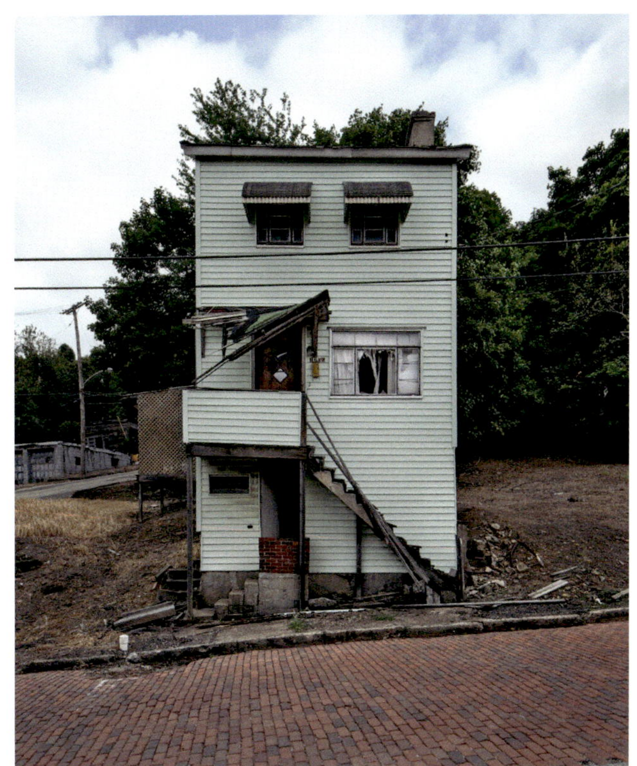

Right: Brick roads feature empty homes with collapsing staircases and roofs.

Below: All that was left of this house was the façade.

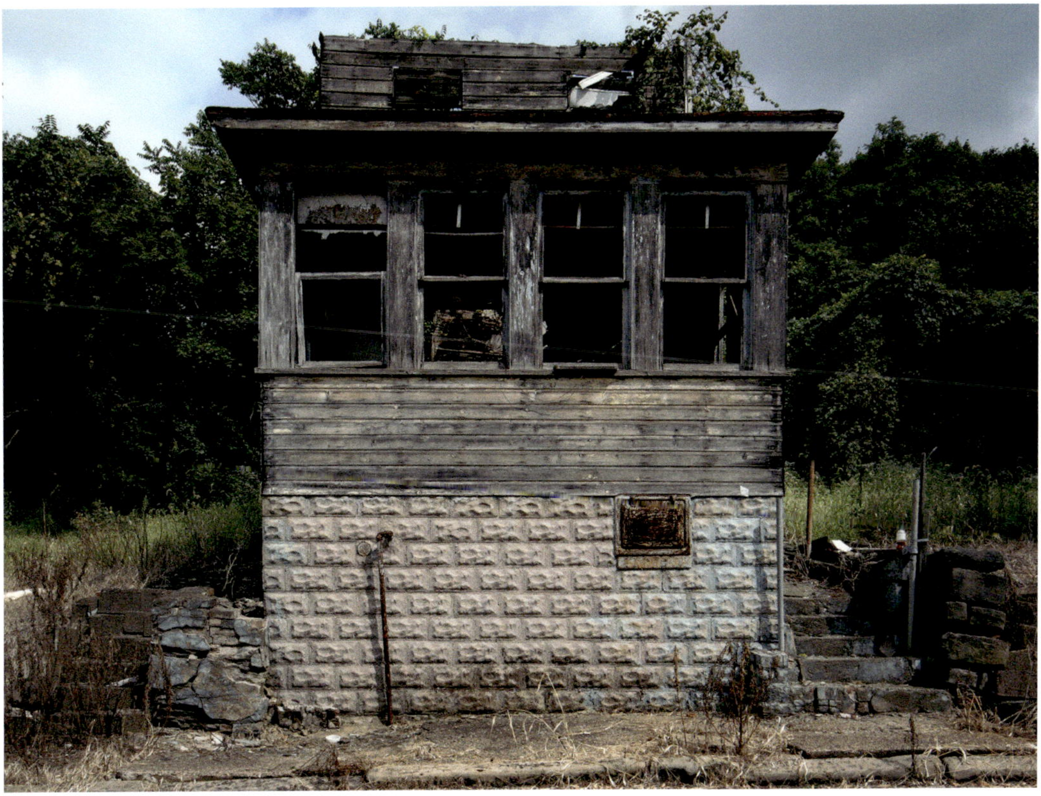

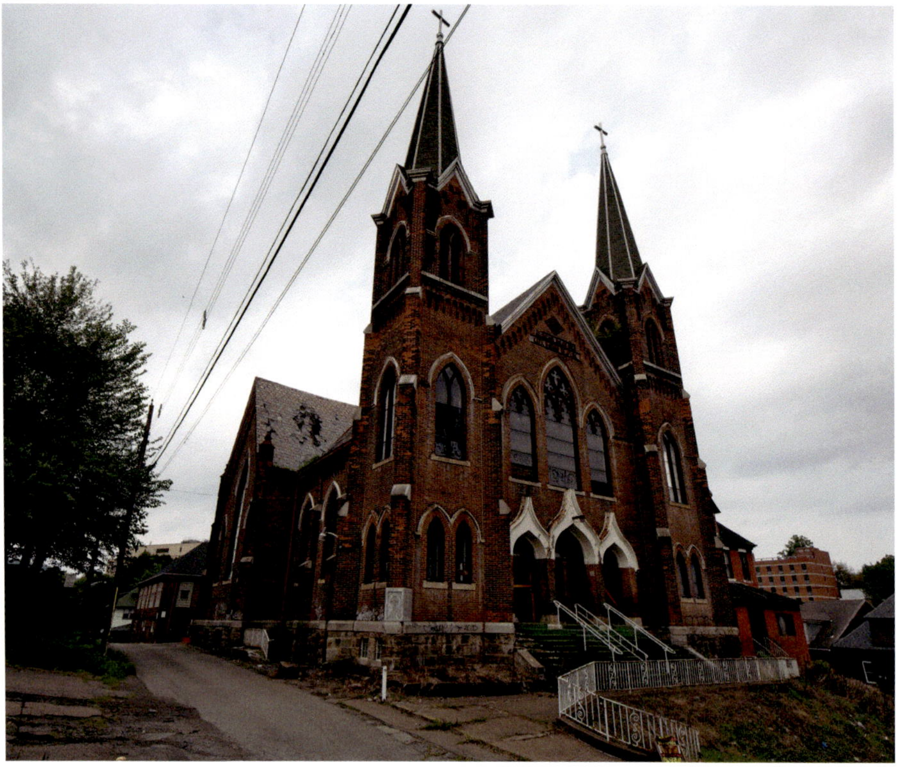

St. Stephen Roman Catholic Magyar Church in McKeesport opened in 1901 and closed in 2002 after the long-standing pastor passed away.

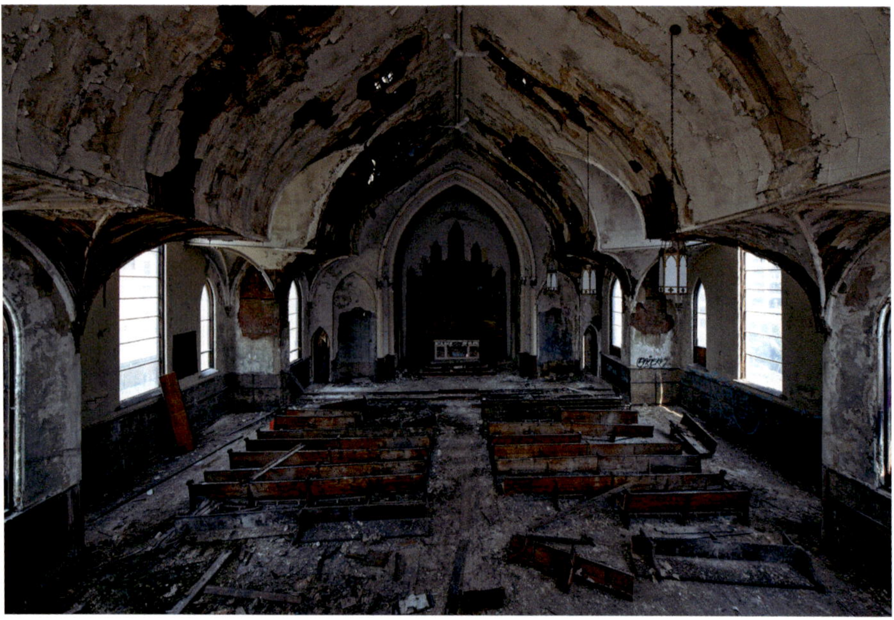

In 2007, the St. Stephen Roman Catholic Magyar Church was purchased by an Italian millionaire Raffaello Follieri. However, the sale was part of an elaborate money laundering scheme. Follieri was sent to federal prison, and St. Stephen's sat abandoned until its demolition in 2020.

8

McKEESPORT PEOPLE'S BANK BUILDING

Built in 1906, the People's Bank Building was originally constructed as an eight-story building shaped like a tower for the People's Union Bank. The building housed twenty-one teller windows on the first floor, with the vault located in the basement. The upper levels were home to dentists, doctors, attorneys, and even the city council. In 1958, the city offices were moved to a different location. Then in 1970, the People's Union bank merged with the Union National Bank of Pittsburgh. In 1993, the building was vacated due to its condition.

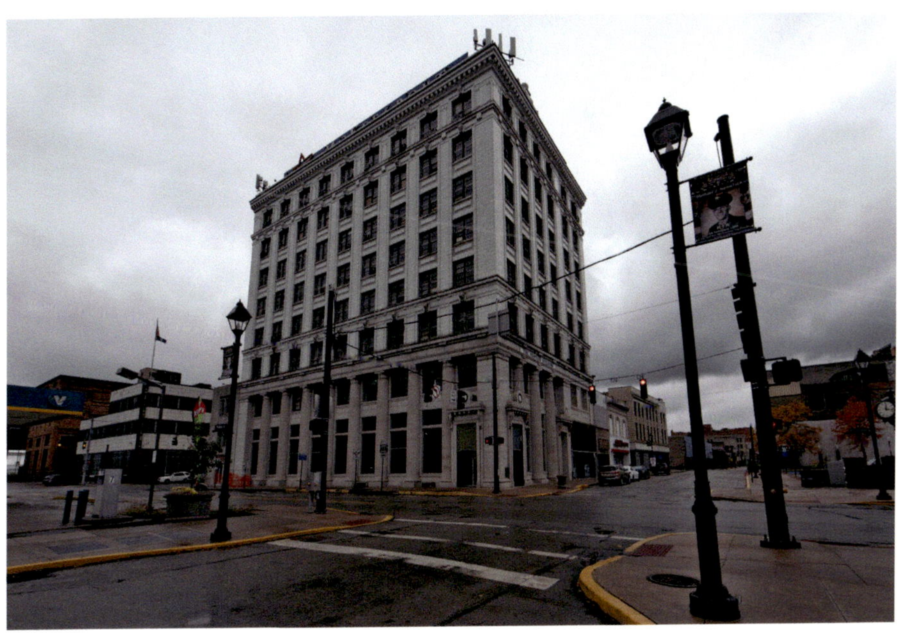

A streetside view of the building.

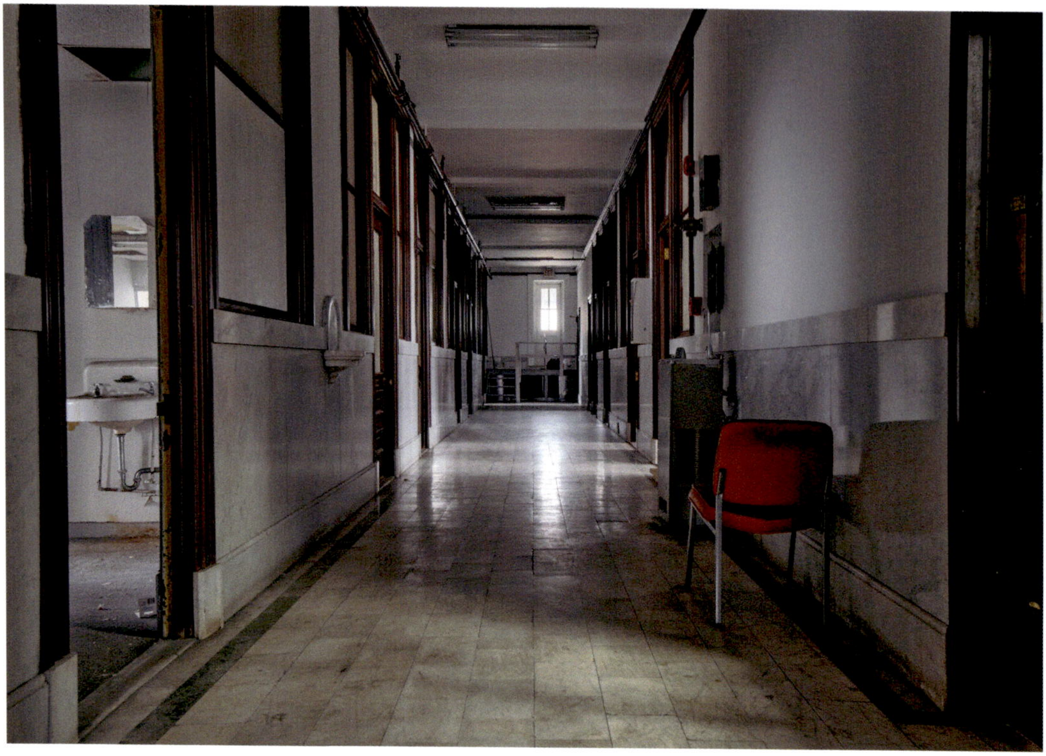

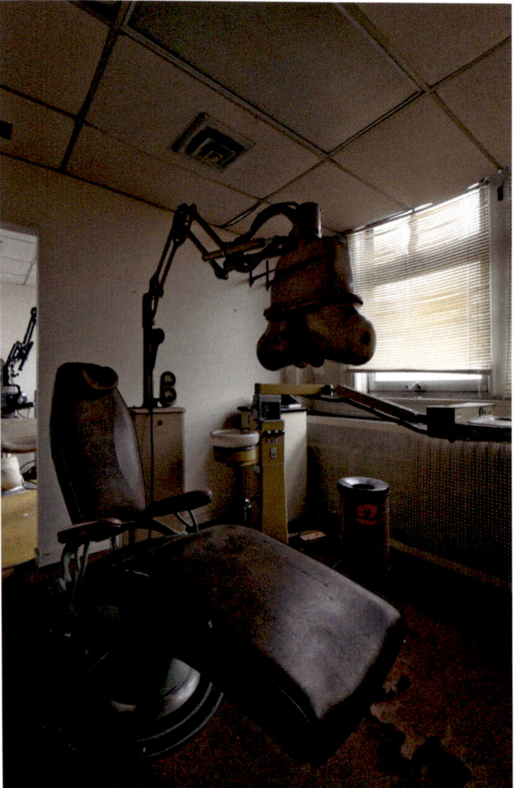

Above: Grand hallways that once held the echoes of people working.

Left: There was a lot of dentist equipment left behind.

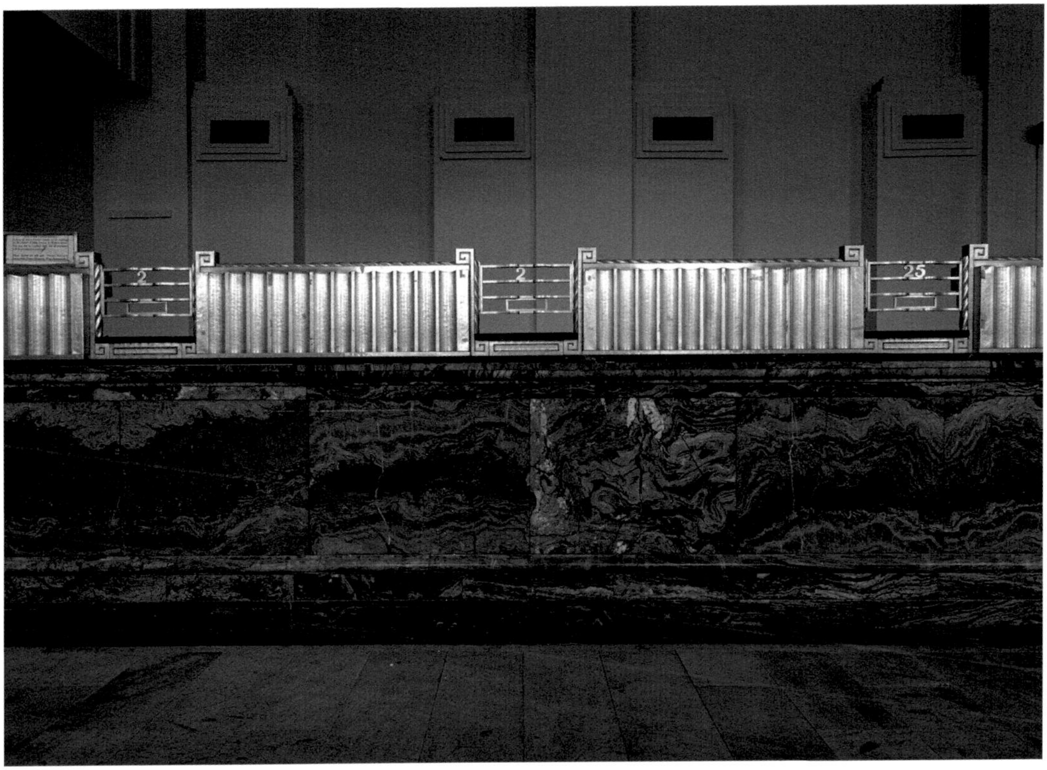

The floors were worn where people frequented the teller windows.

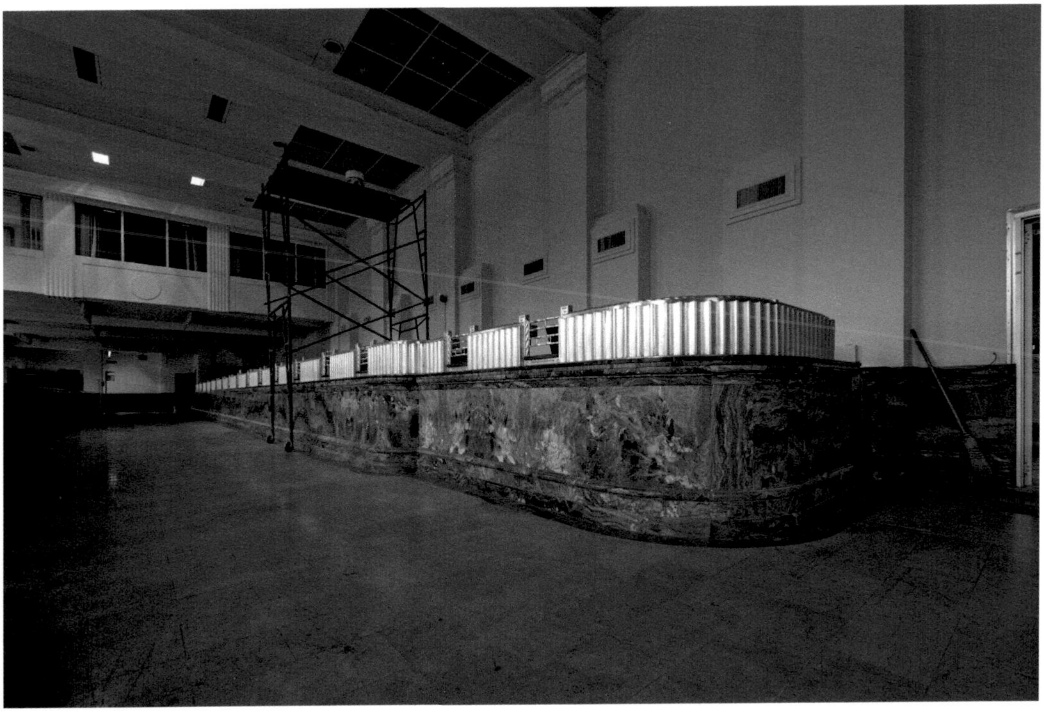

Work had begun during my visit to bring the main lobby back to its glory.

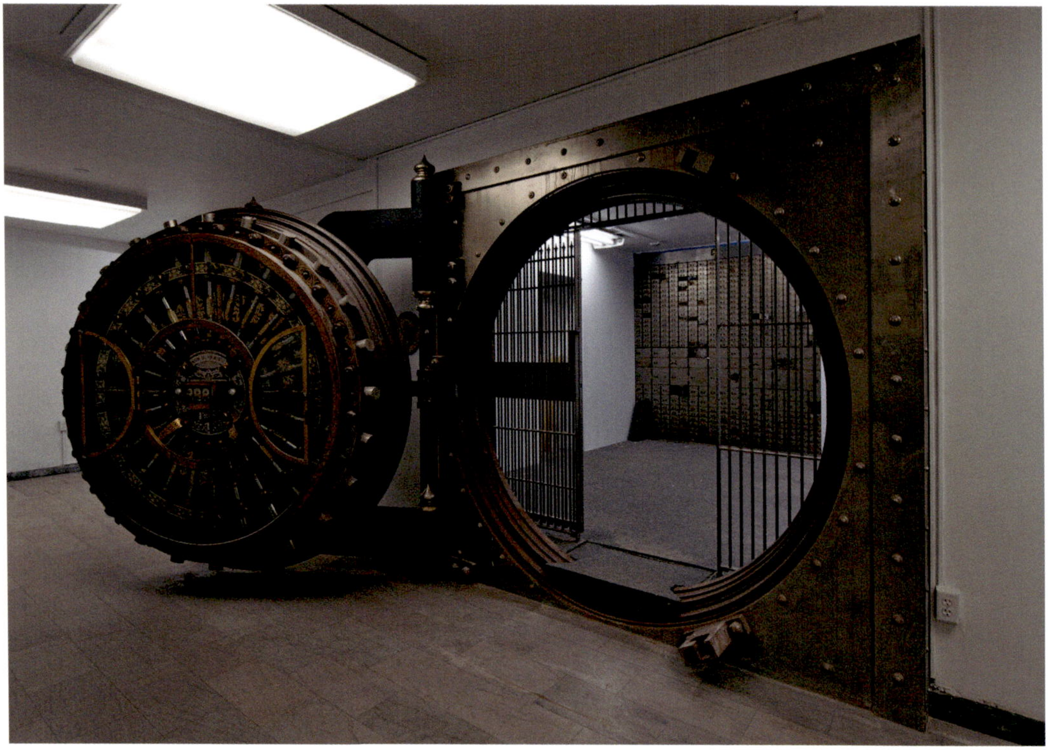

The owner told me that the vault was moved to the basement at some point.

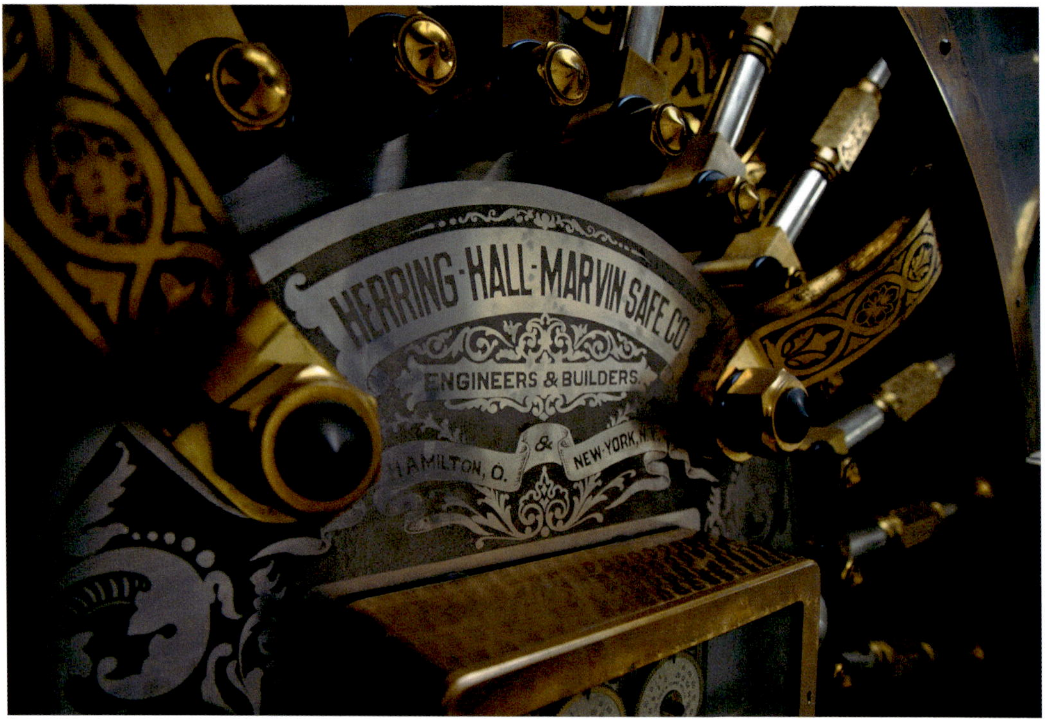

Fine detail of the vault constructed by the Herring-Hall-Marvin Safe company of Hamilton, Ohio, and New York City, New York.

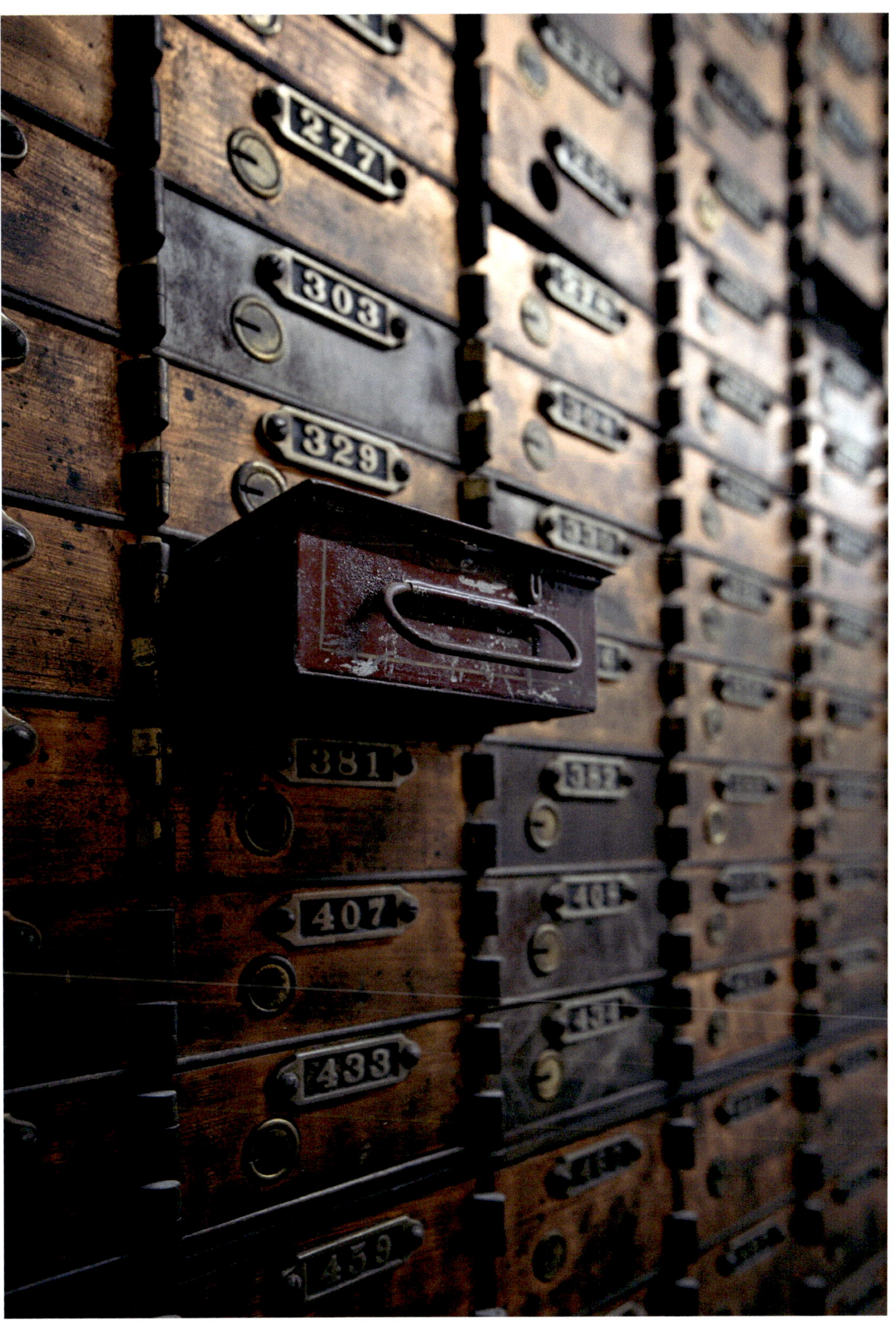

A safety deposit box stuck sticking out. I wonder if anything was left inside.

9

MILES BRYAN HIGH SCHOOL

The school was built in 1927 out of large bricks. It has unique terraced grounds and has an incredible view of the Pittsburgh skyline. Located in Mckees Rocks, Pennsylvania, the school was named in honor of Justice of the Peace Miles Bryan. On January 29, 1928, the Miles Bryan High School opened its doors to its first graduating class. Mckees Rocks merged with the Stowe school district in 1966, and the high school became a middle school. Like many other cities along the Ohio River, Mckees Rocks fell to disrepair in the 1980s, causing much of the population to relocate. The school closed its doors in 1997. The abandoned school was sold to a developer in 2001. Even with plans to convert the school into housing, nothing has been done with the school, and it sits in poor condition.

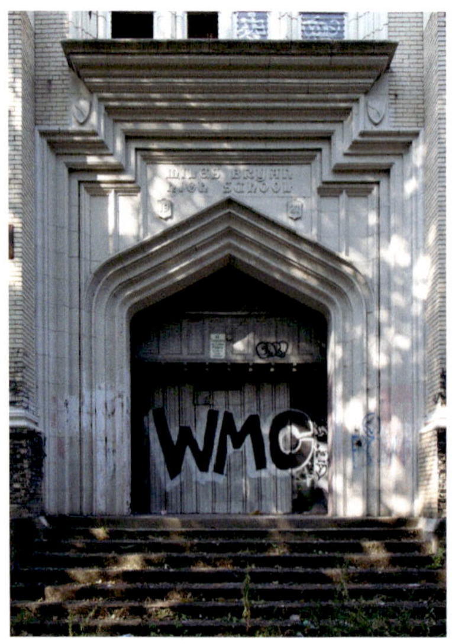

Above the school's front entrance, its name was uniquely designed and carved into the brick.

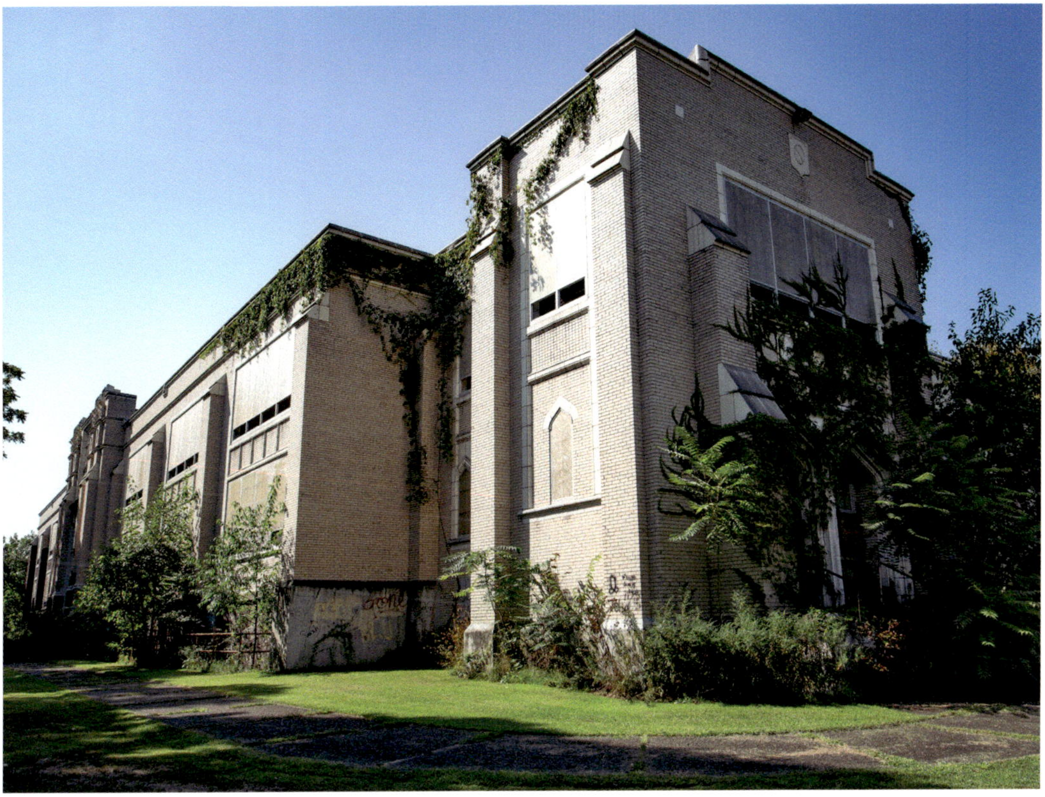

Taken in the late summer of 2016, you can see much of the school's landscaping had begun to grow wild and even climb the sides of the school.

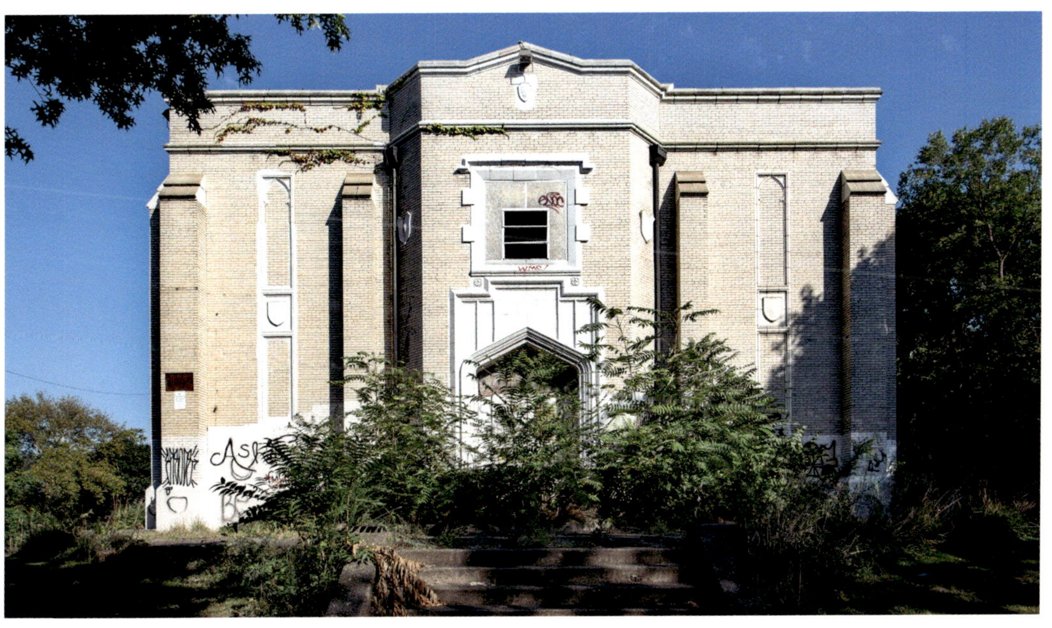

The school had a unique design with intricate detail.

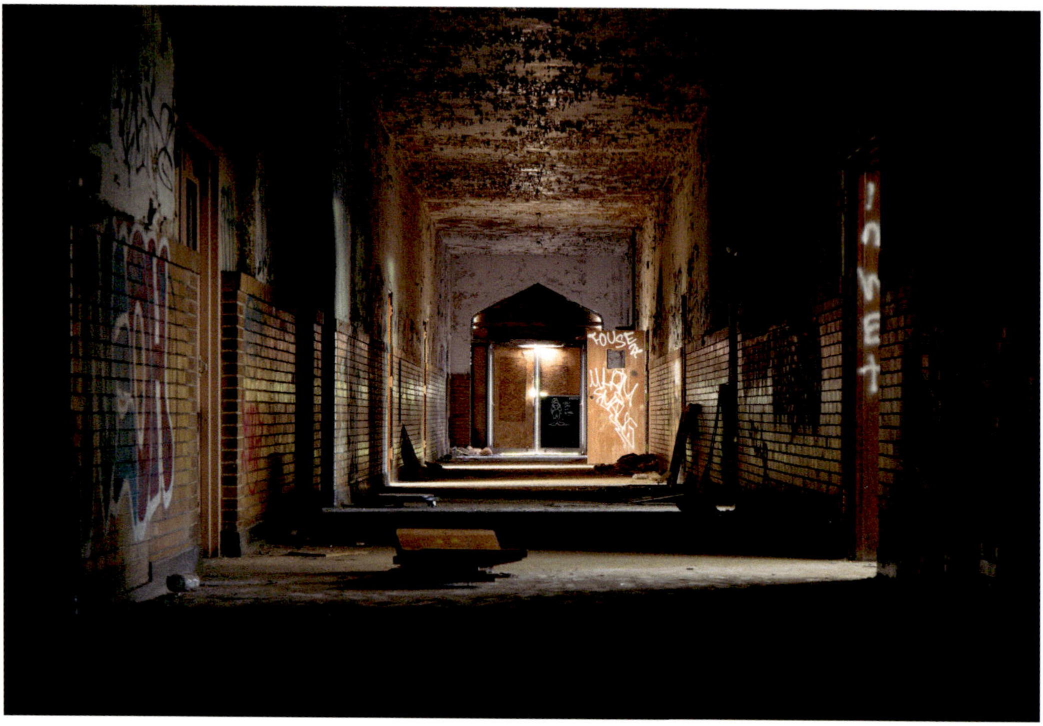

A hallway on the first floor with an odd-shaped archway.

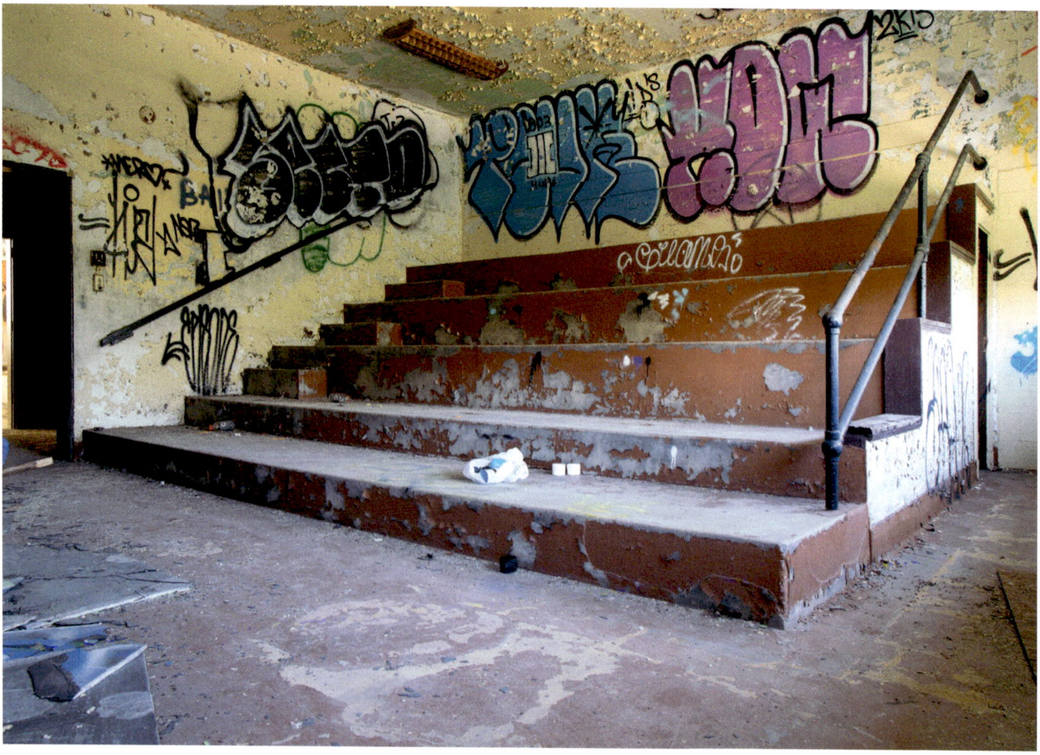

Almost all of the classrooms contained graffiti.

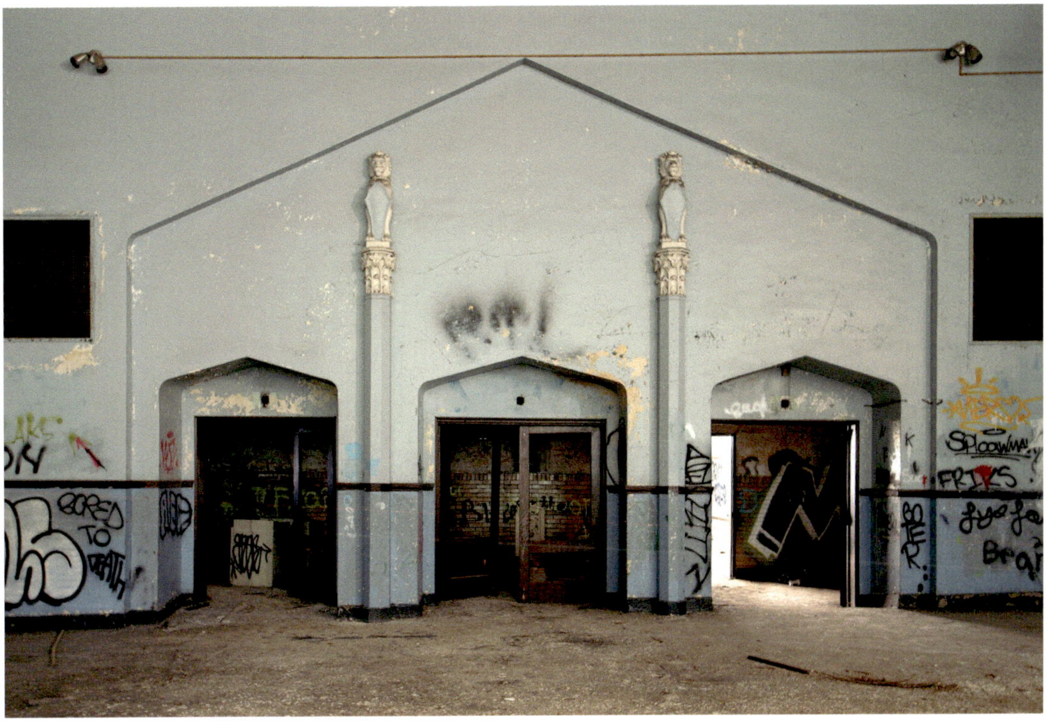

The entrances that lead into the auditorium.

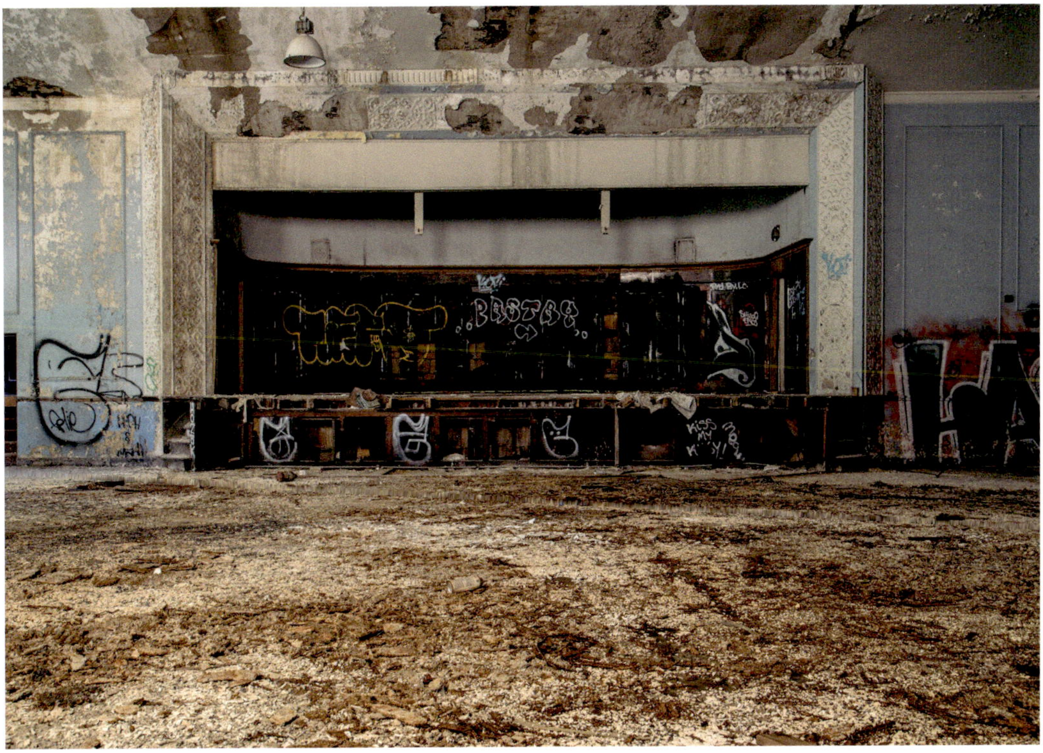

The auditorium stage was destroyed and full of graffiti.

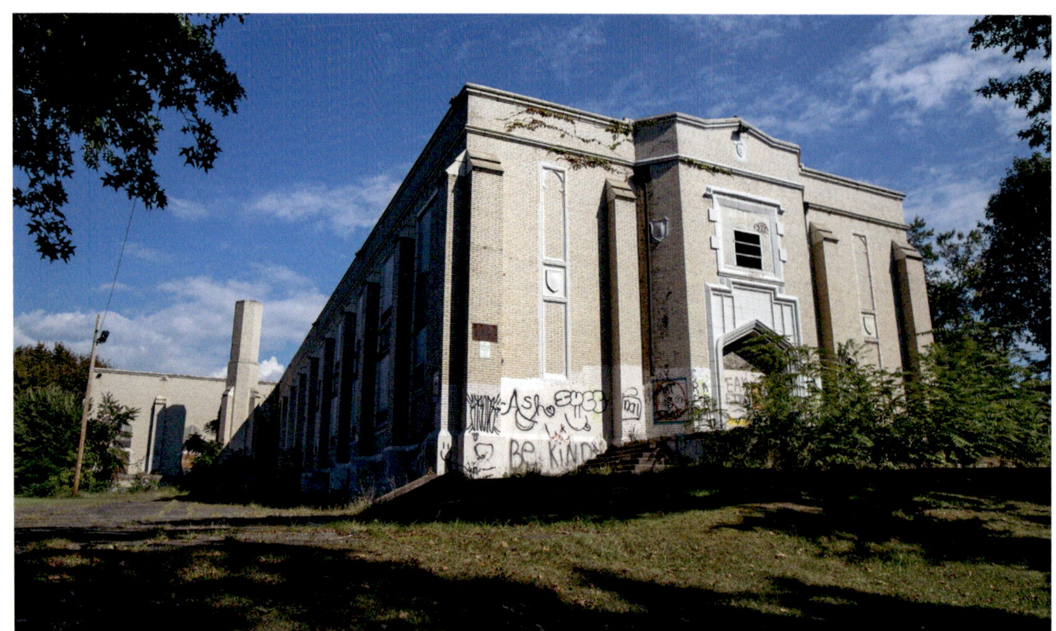

A broken basement window was the only way into the school. You had to climb into the dark, not knowing if anyone was there or what you were climbing into.

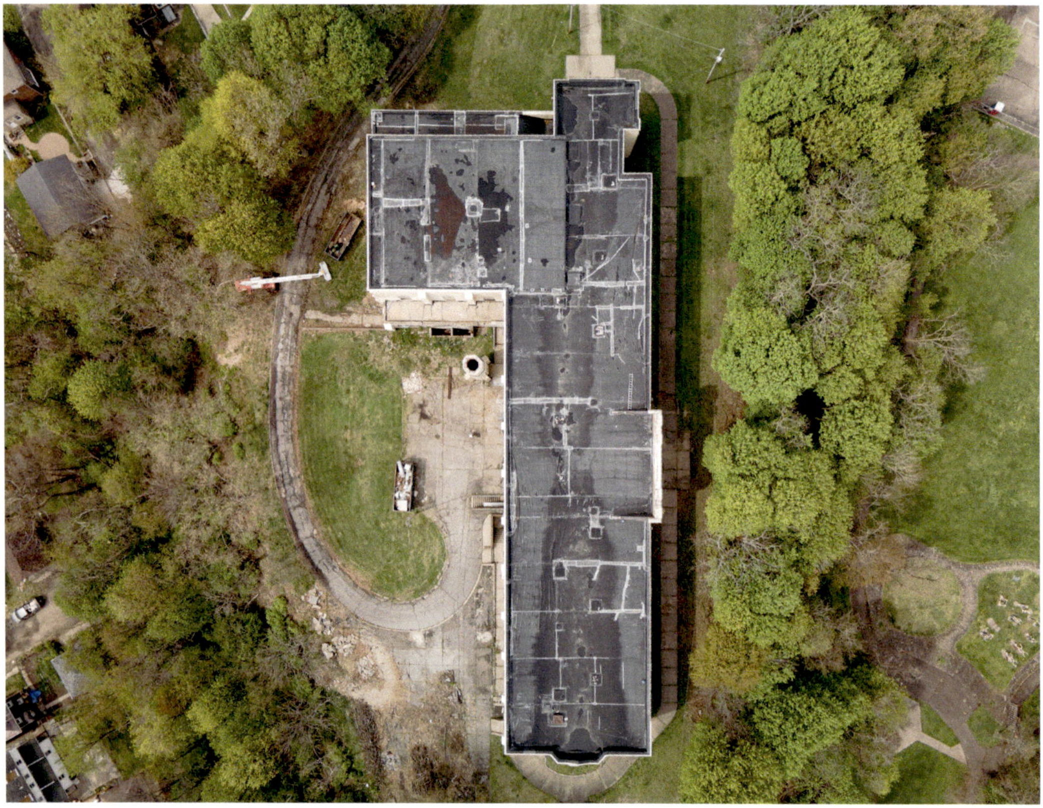

A bird's eye view of the school taken in 2021 shows they have begun cleaning the school out.

10

THE CITY OF MONESSEN

Monessen, like McKeesport, for four decades has lost half of its population. There are many abandoned homes, schools, churches, and buildings left in ruins in the city. After talking with a local official, I was able to find out that Monessen has around 400 abandoned properties. While they have made many efforts to bring life back to the city, it is a slow process.

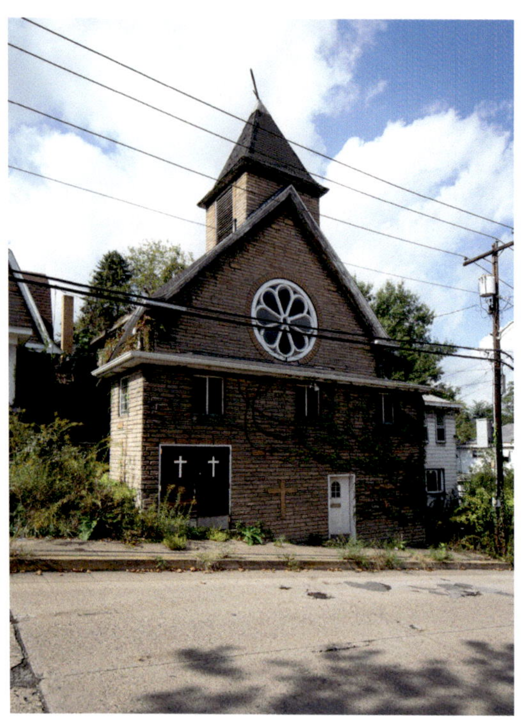

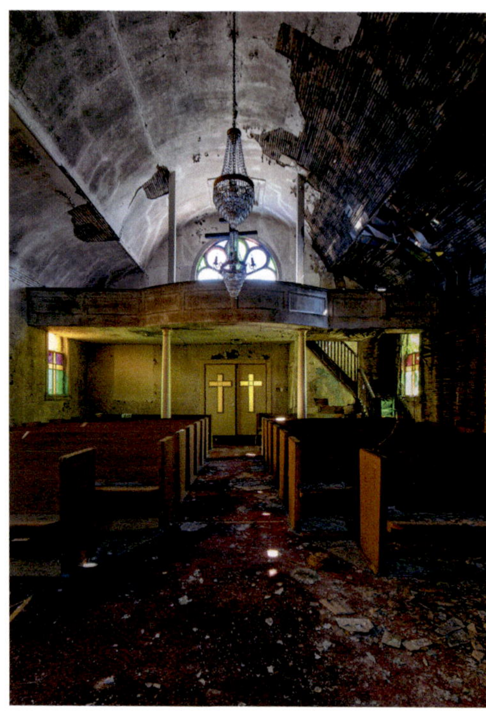

Above left: An old church tucked away, hidden on a busy street.

Above right: Decay begins to take over the church chapel.

Right: Vines are covering an empty home.

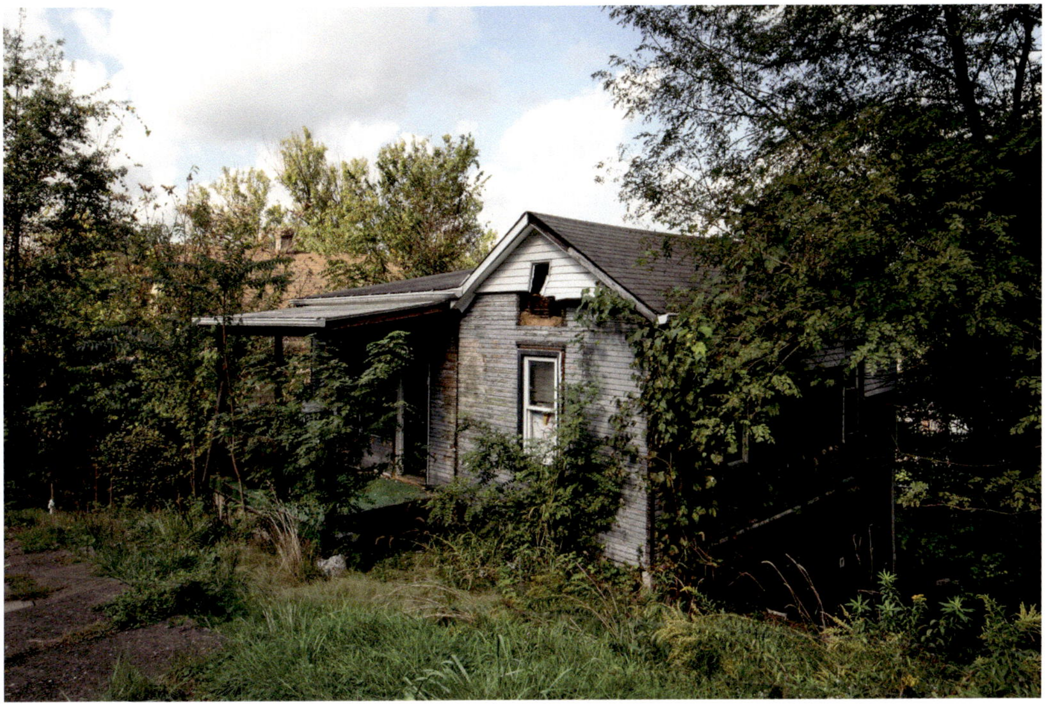

Above: The door was wide open on this house. Fascinated by the outside, I never thought to peek inside.

Right: Many streets are lined with empty homes.

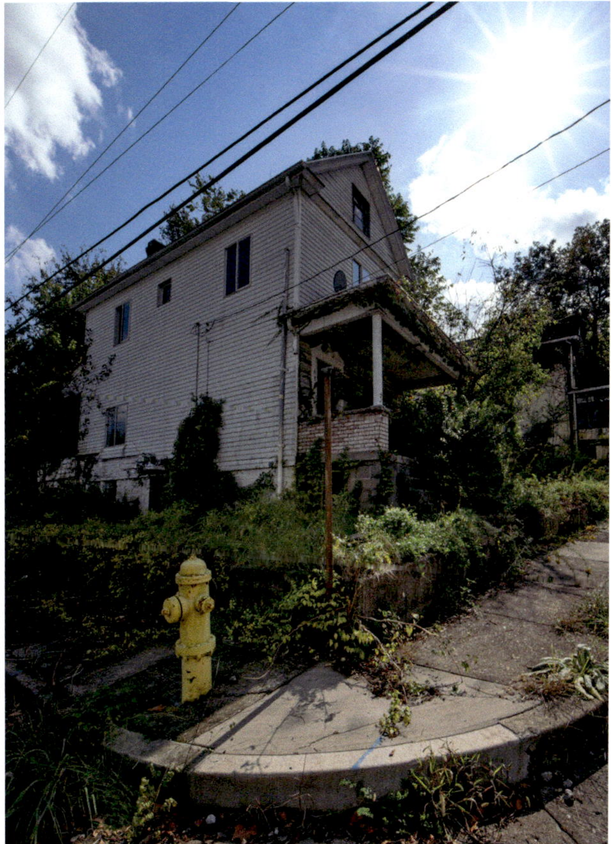

11

MONONGAHELA HOTEL

The Monongahela hotel was built in 1925. The building consists of four stories containing 143 rooms. The hotel was initially known as the Monongahela House. When the town declined, the hotel was used as college dorms. The hotel was bought by Frank Bock, who renamed the hotel the Towne Hotel, and it was converted into apartments. The hotel has sat vacant since the 1990s. The reasons for the closure of the hotel are not publicly known.

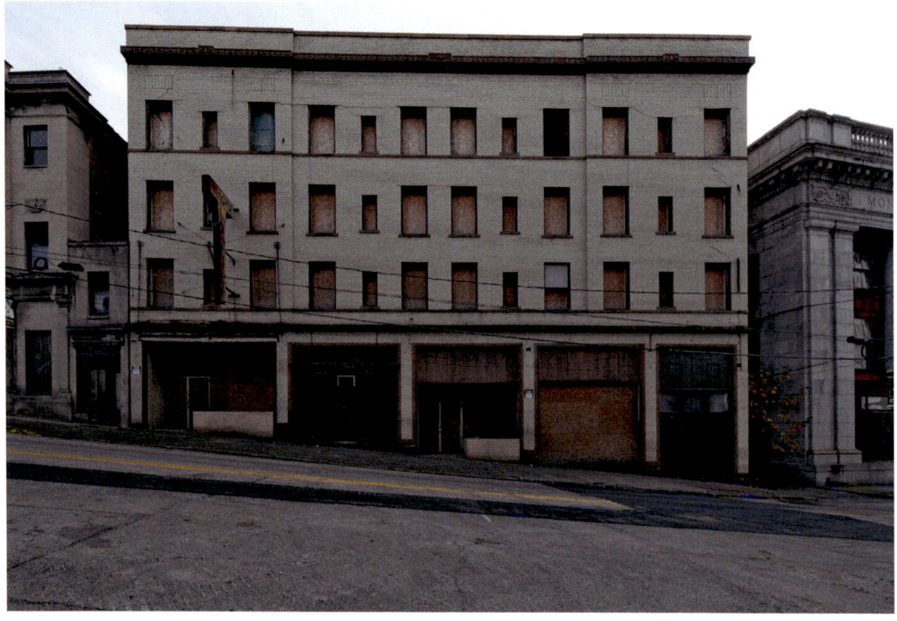

A view of the hotel in front of the old train station.

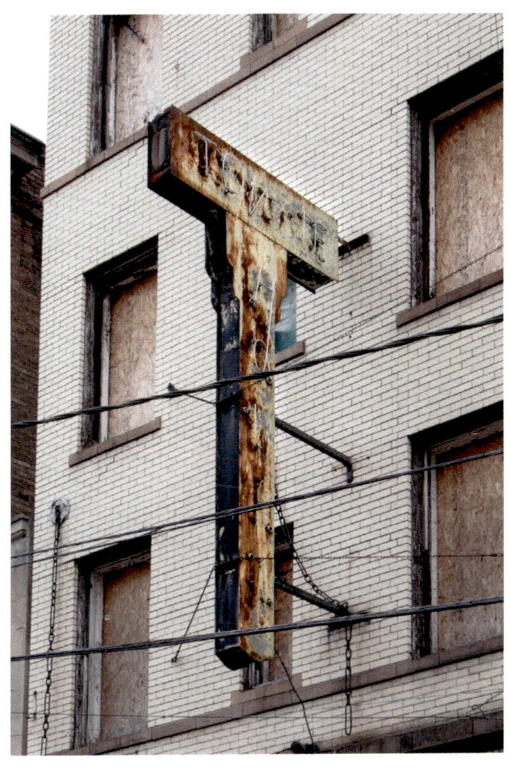

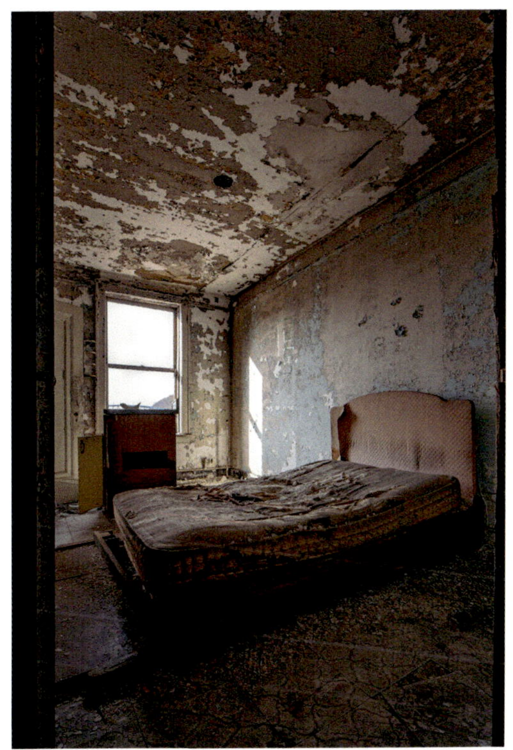

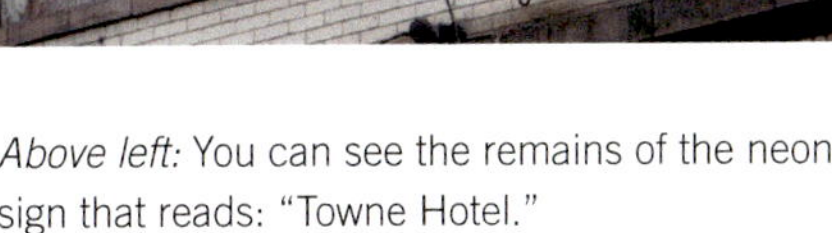

Above left: You can see the remains of the neon sign that reads: "Towne Hotel."

Above right: An old bed begins to fall apart.

Right: Ceiling debris litters the floor of a long hallway.

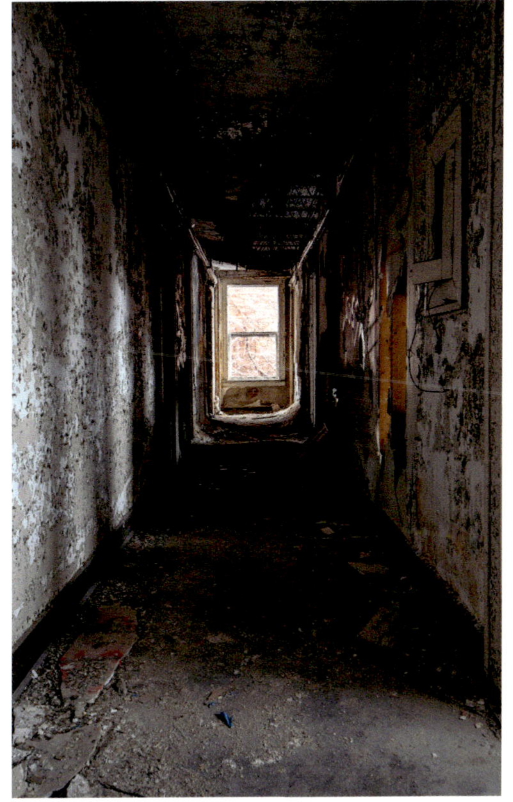

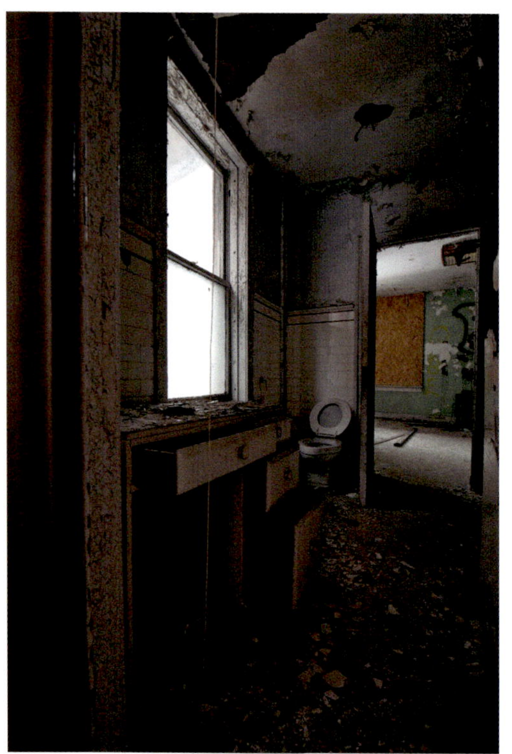

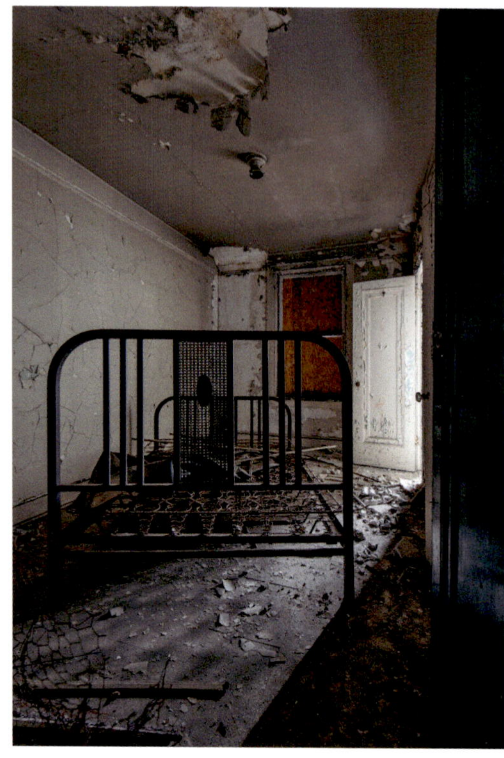

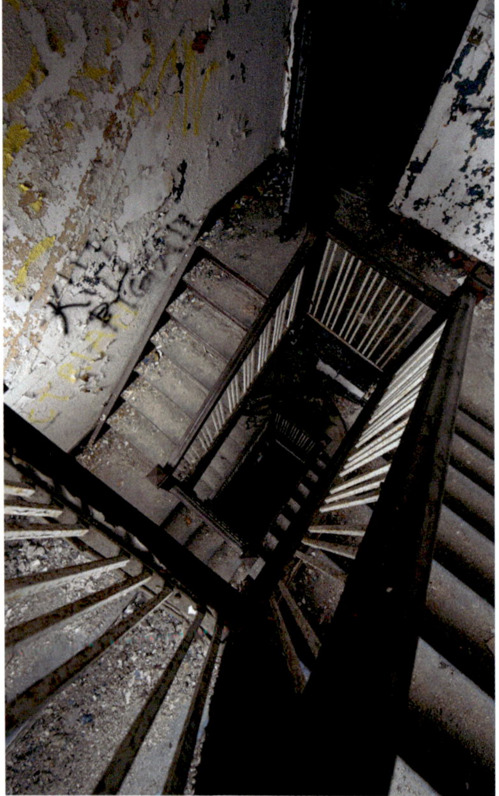

Above left: Many of the rooms had connecting bathrooms.

Above right: A bed frame with a mattress that has been stripped completely of its fabric and fibers.

Left: A winding staircase that leads to a blackout basement.

12

NATIONAL NEGRO OPERA COMPANY HOUSE

The National Negro Opera Company was the United States' first African American opera company. Organized in Pittsburgh, Pennsylvania, the company was founded in 1941. Mary Cardwell Dawson, a classically trained opera singer, rented the third floor of the house located in Homewood to use as an office and rehearsal space. The company was successful, traveling to major cities in the U.S. to perform. For twenty-one years, Mary Dawson trained students in jazz piano, voice, and classical music. In 1962, the company closed its doors when Dawson passed away, and the company was disbanded. The Queen Anne-style house was believed to have been built in the late 1800s. Today, the seventeen-room structure is on the verge of collapse. The National Trust for Historic Preservation has included the house on its most endangered sites list. The property was purchased in 2000, which saved it from demolition; however, no work has been done to preserve the structure. The owner hopes to restore the property and has been raising funds to begin renovations.

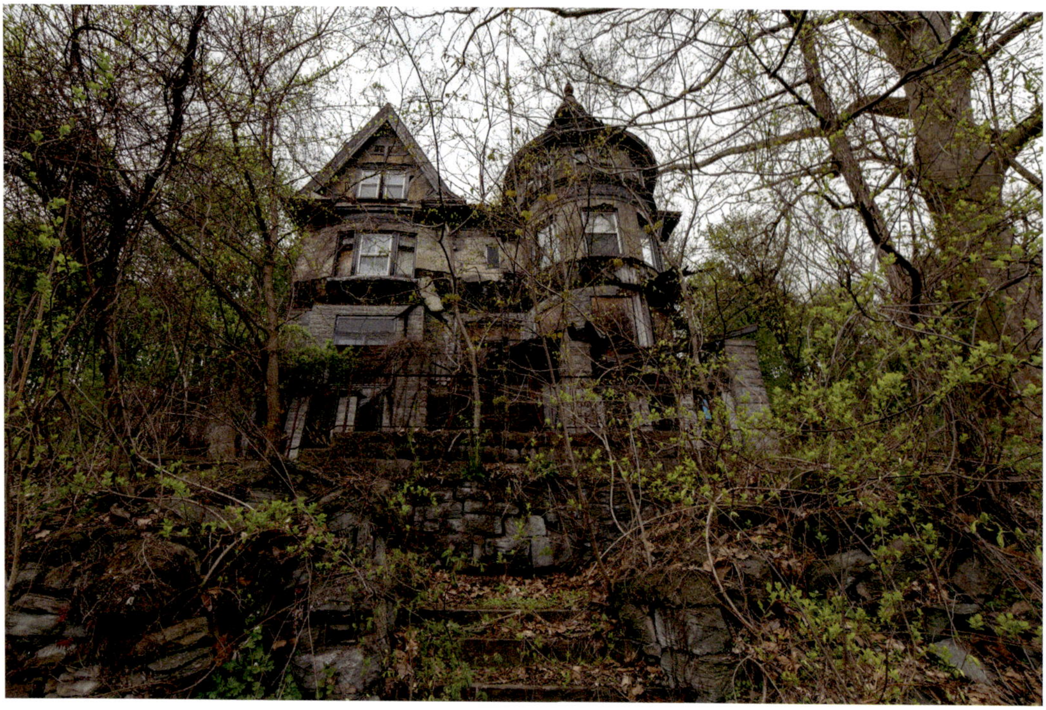

A photo taken from the road shows that the house sits up on an incline.

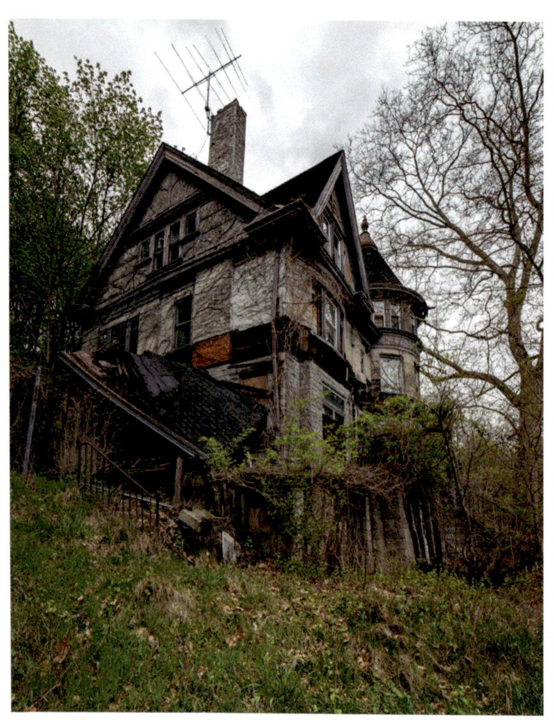

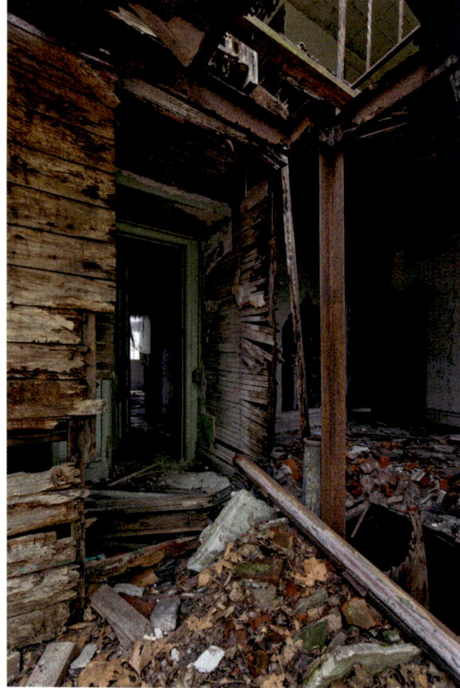

Above left: A side view of the house shows a collapsed roof.

Above right: The house was falling apart and left exposed to the elements.

13

SHENANGO CHINA

The Shenango China Company was incorporated in 1901. Shenango China made dinnerware and semi-vitreous hotel ware. A plant was built in New Castle, Pennsylvania, on Emery Street. Shenango China fell victim to financial difficulty in 1905, just four years after incorporating. Due to this difficulty, a receiver was appointed, and a charter was taken out under the name of Shenango Pottery Company. In 1912, Shenango China purchased the New Castle Pottery Company plant and moved its equipment to the new location. The flood of 1913 delayed the opening of the new plant due to 3 feet of water covering the plant. The plant opened officially in May 1913. The company made commercial china for restaurants, hotels, and institutions until 1935. From 1936 to 1958, Shenango made china for Theodore Haviland Company.

In 1979, the plant was sold to Anchor Hocking Corporation of Lancaster, Ohio. Then in 1987, Hocking sold the plant to the Newell Company of Freeport, Illinois. Just six months later, the plant was sold to Syracuse China. Syracuse China made the decision to close the plant and reorganize. All employees were left jobless and had to reapply for their previous positions. Many of them were denied their positions back. Syracuse China sold Shenango to Pfaltzgraff Company of York, PA, in 1989. An economic downturn resulted in consolidation and contributed to the closing of the Shenango plant. The company remained in business until December 1991.

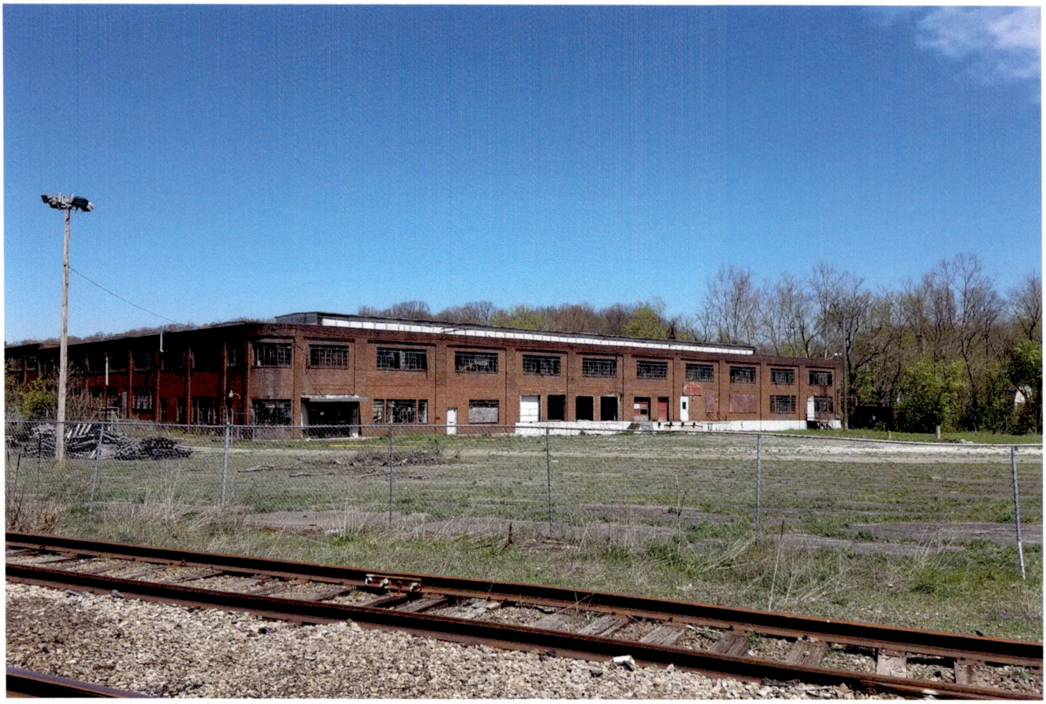

A street view of the factory.

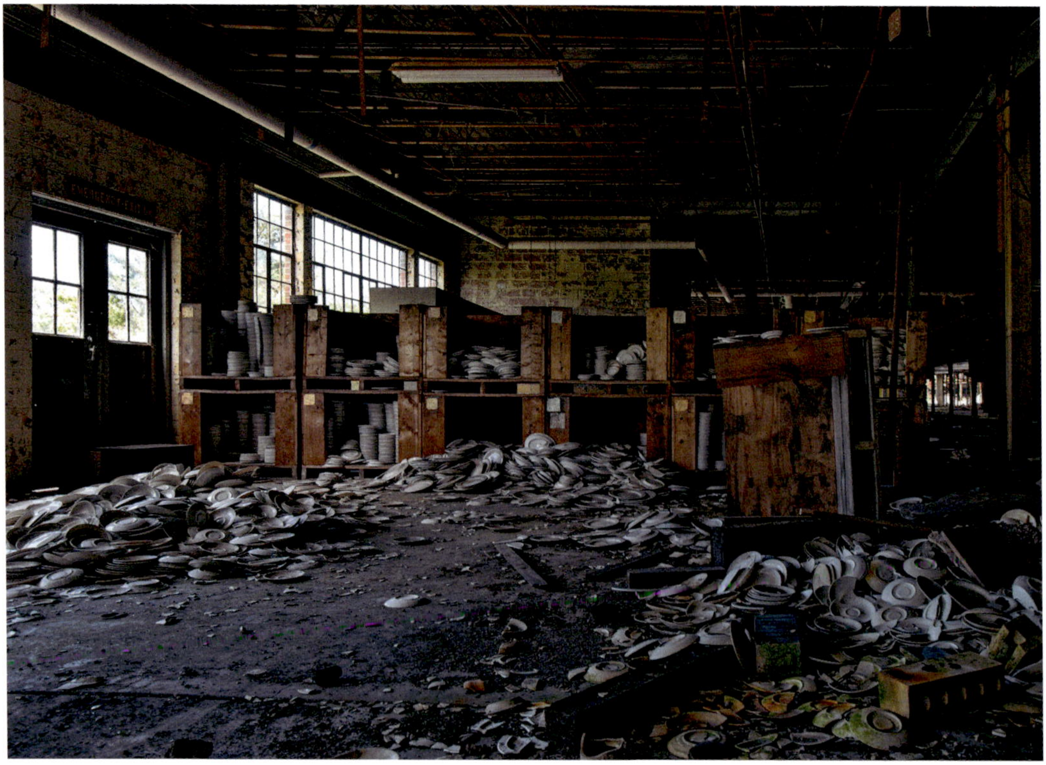

China plates have begun to slide off the pallets and break.

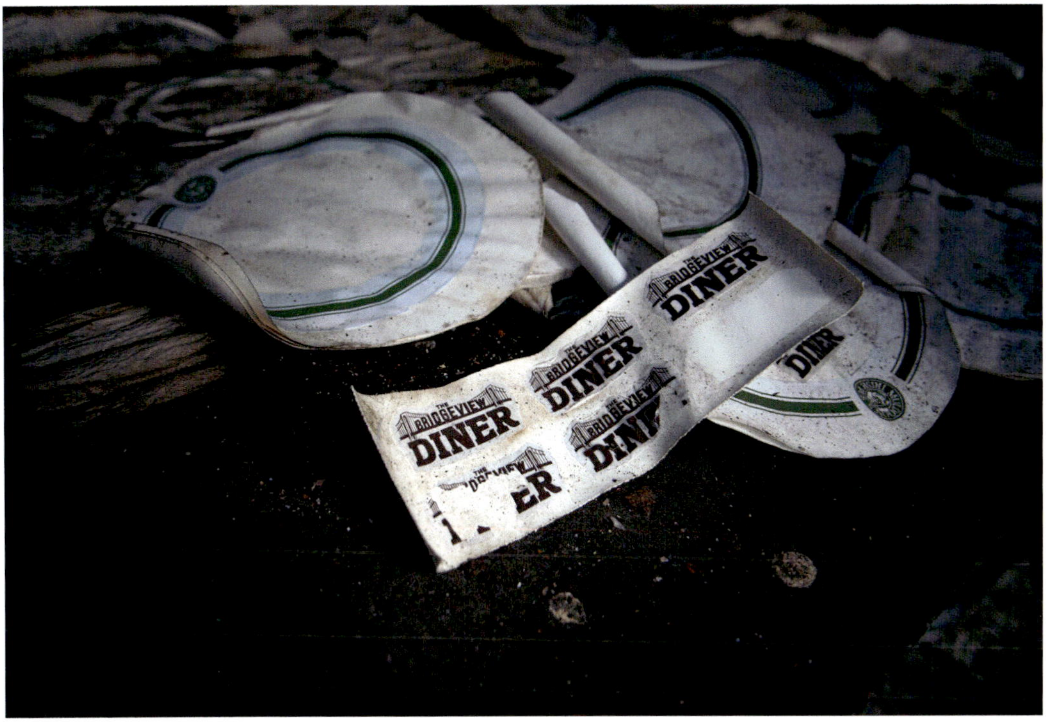

Unused transfer-print designs left stacked on a table. The Bridgeview Diner is still open today in Brooklyn, New York.

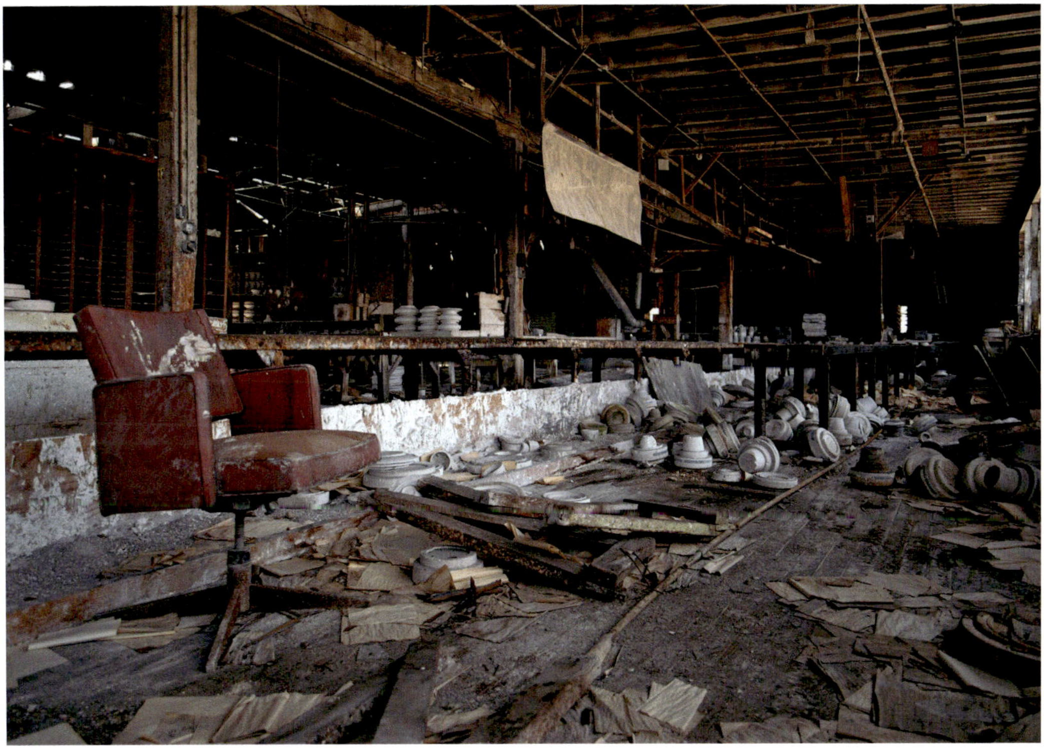

What appears to have been an assembly line of some sort rusts away, and molds have fallen to the ground.

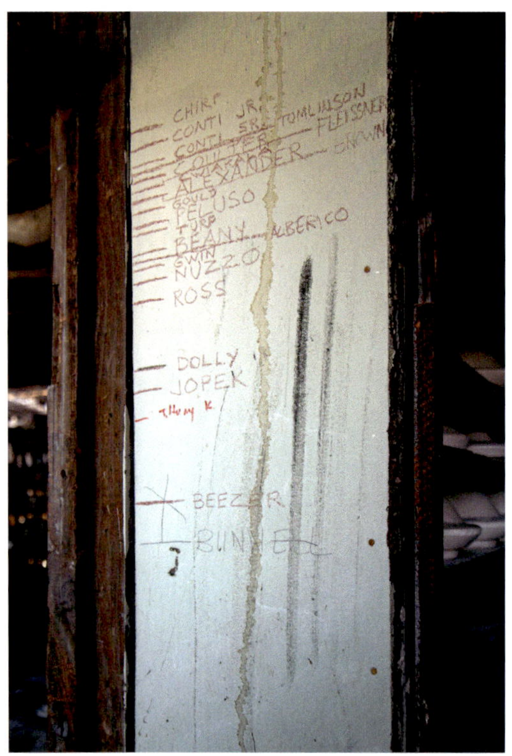

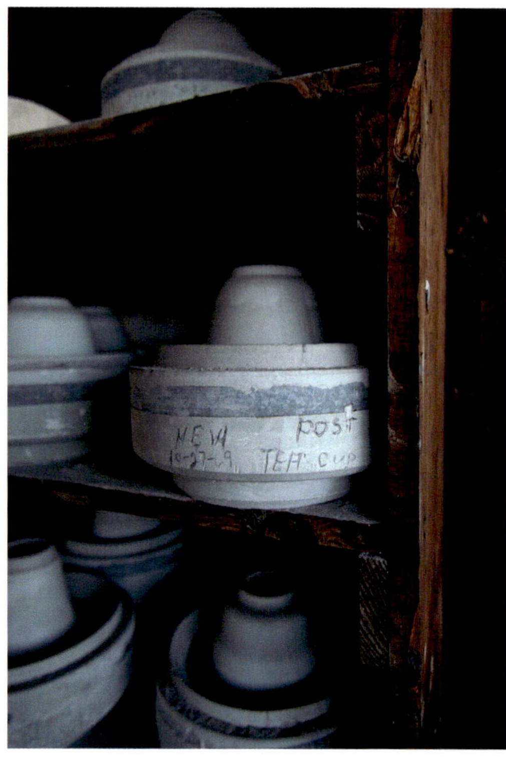

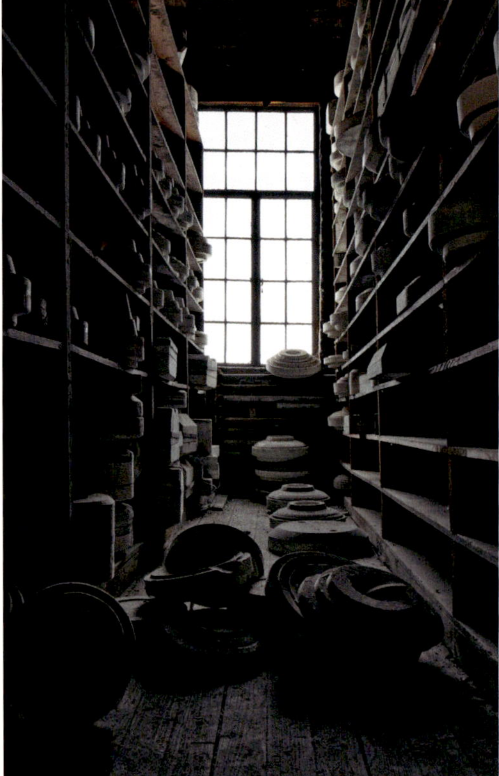

Above left: One of the doorways had markings with names. Unsure if this was measuring height or production, it was still a unique find.

Above right: A teacup mold sits on a shelf in perfect condition. It makes you wonder how many cups this single mold created before it was decommissioned.

Left: China molds stacked on shelves that stretch to the ceiling.

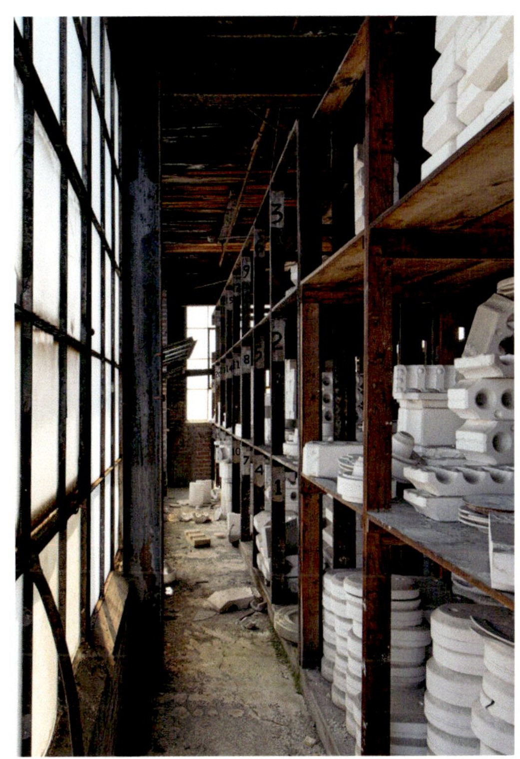

Right: Numbers on the shelves leave clues of the remains of an old organizational system.

Below: Moss grows on the floors of what appears to be a workshop.

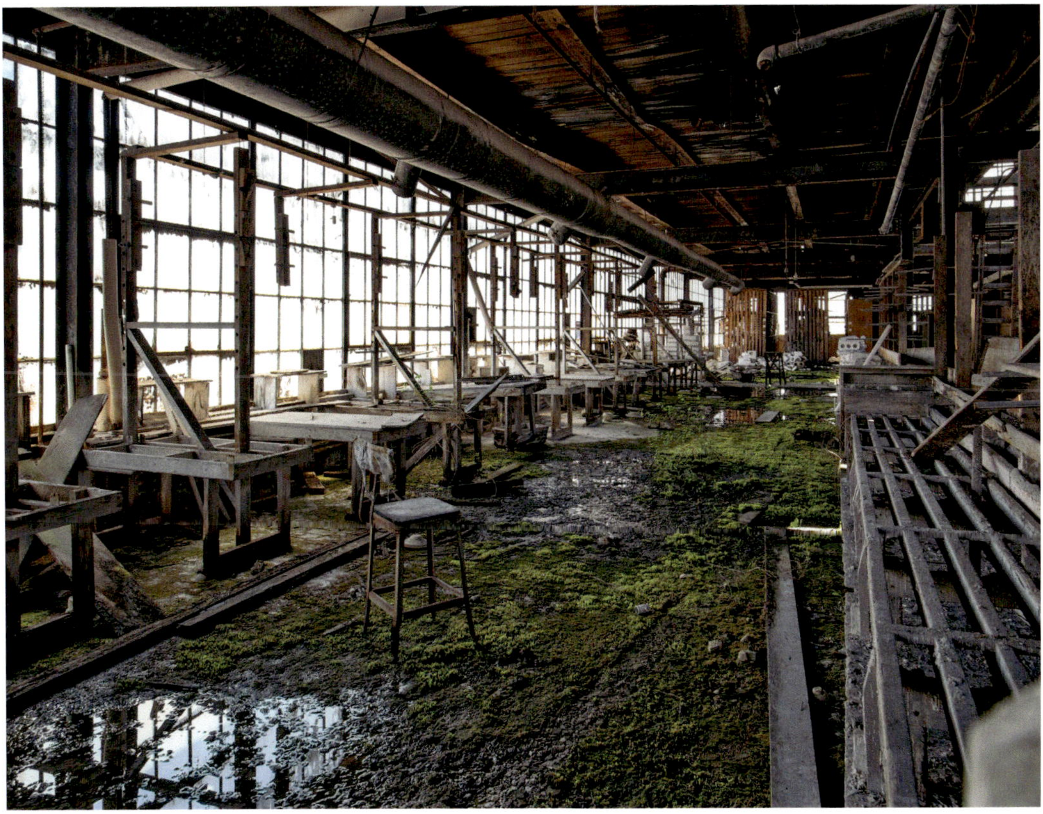

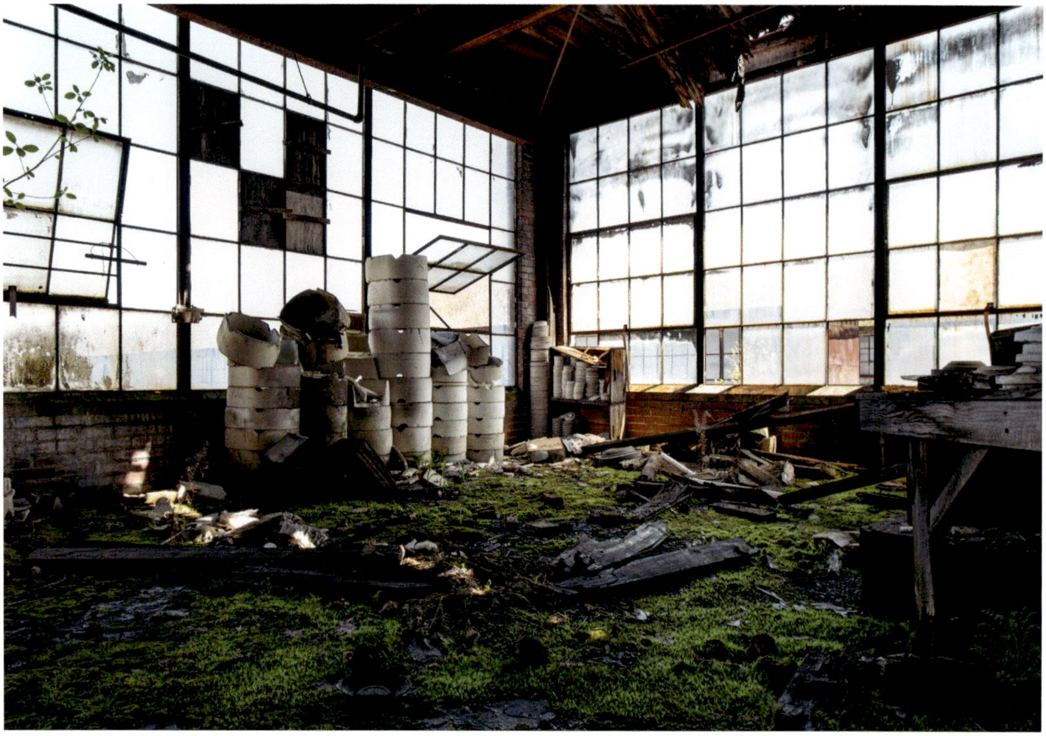

Extensive water damage has begun the beginning stages of the roof's decay.

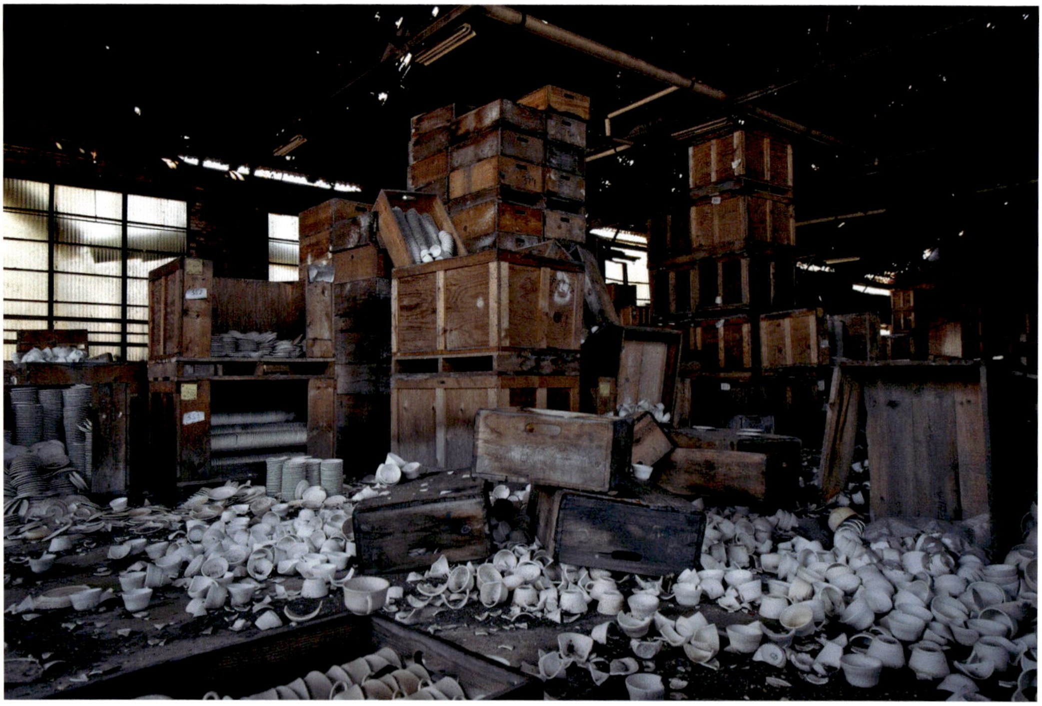

Many pallets were labeled and ready for shipment. As water damage weakens the pallets, many cups and plates are destroyed as they fall to the floor.

14

STATE CORRECTIONAL INSTITUTION (SCI) CRESSON

SCI Cresson, located in Cambria County, was originally the Cresson Sanatorium. Cresson Sanatorium was built in 1913 and was one of the first tuberculosis sanatoriums. In the early nineteenth century, tuberculosis was one of the leading causes of death, with one in every seven people dying from the infection. A doctor in Germany had discovered that tuberculosis was contagious, which led to the confinement of people in sanatoriums to treat the disease. As new treatments and drugs emerged, tuberculosis patients lessened, and the need for sanatoriums declined. The sanatorium was renamed Lawrence F. Flick State Hospital in 1956. The Department of Public Welfare ran the Lawrence F. Flick State Hospital, which treated developmentally disabled patients.

The administration building underwent renovation in 1962. In 1964, the facility became Cresson State School and Hospital. The hospital underwent another name change in 1970 to Cresson Center before changing hands with the Department of Corrections. An executive order by Governor Dick Thornburgh in 1983 transferred the property to the Bureau of Corrections. The renovation of the hospital to design new housing units for inmates cost $20.6 million. Many of the original structures of the hospital were left intact. In 1987, SCI Cresson opened as a medium-security correction facility for men. The prison housed up to 1,600 prisoners. The prison operated until June 30, 2013, following the announcement of its closure in January of that year. Most of the buildings sat unused, but the property was managed by a caretaker. In 2016, a $600,000 bid by Carl Weaver was placed on SCI Cresson. The state accepted an offer from the logging company who wanted to remove hardwoods. When the work was complete, the property was actually abandoned. Today, Big House Produce has repurposed the property and uses the buildings for their hydroponic company.

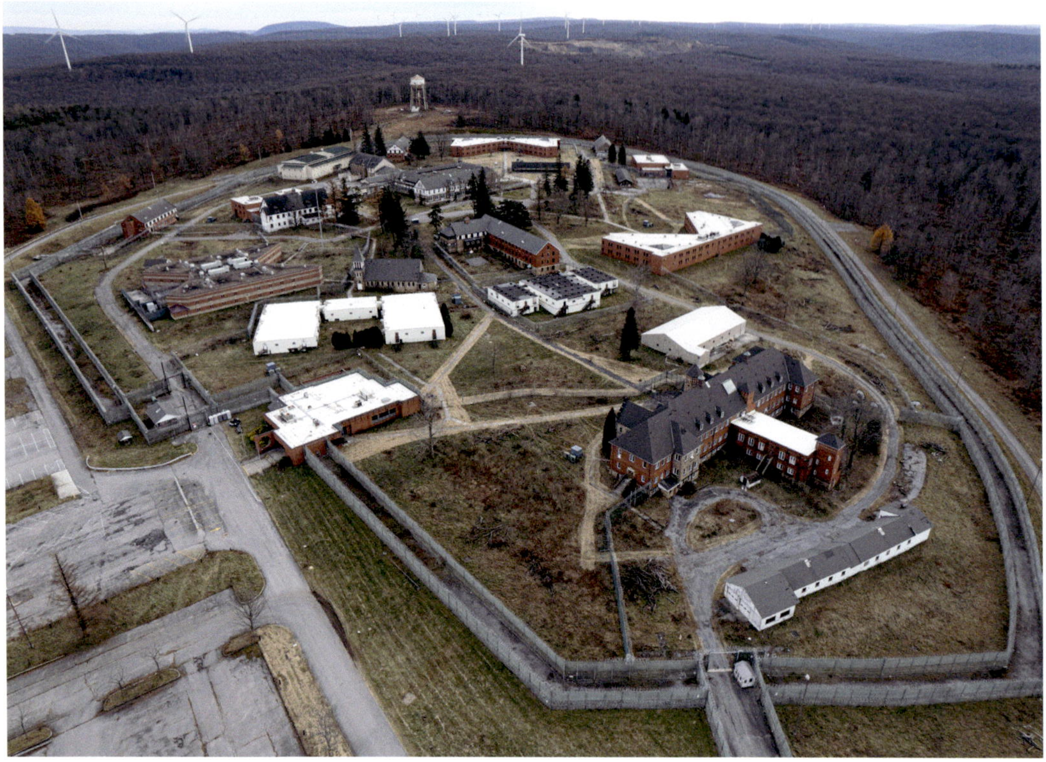

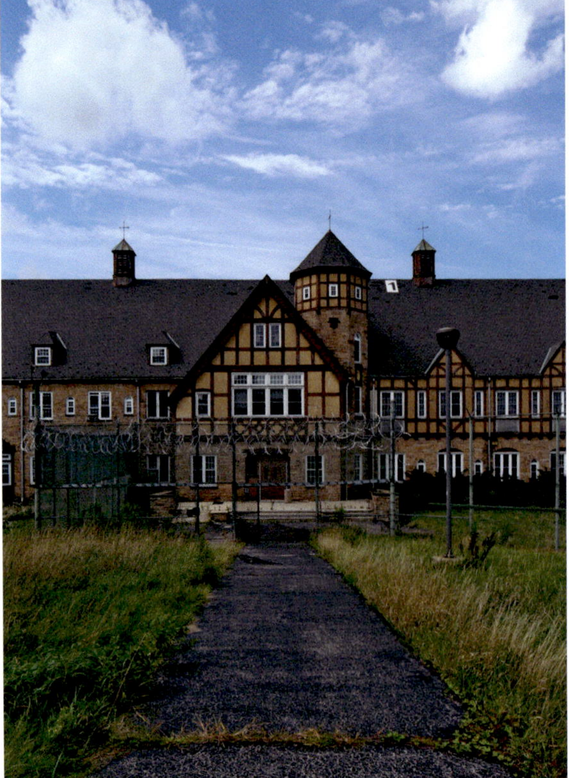

Above: The vast property is home to many buildings.

Left: This building, known as the Maple House School, was used for administrative and educational purposes.

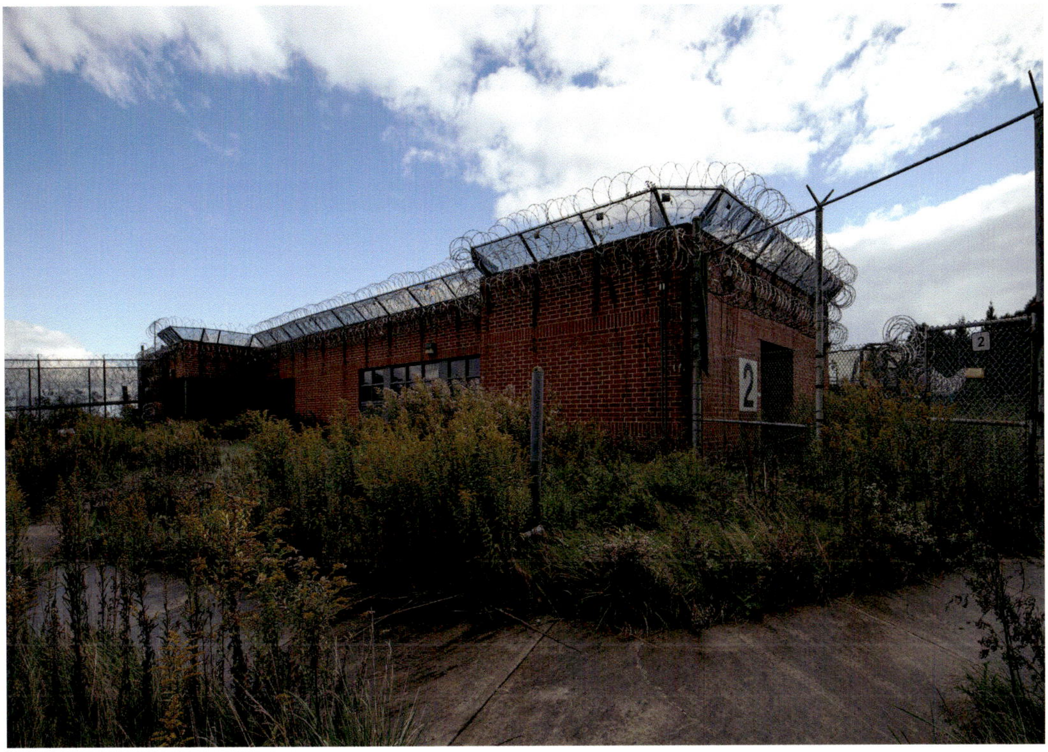

Visitors' building for the prisoners.

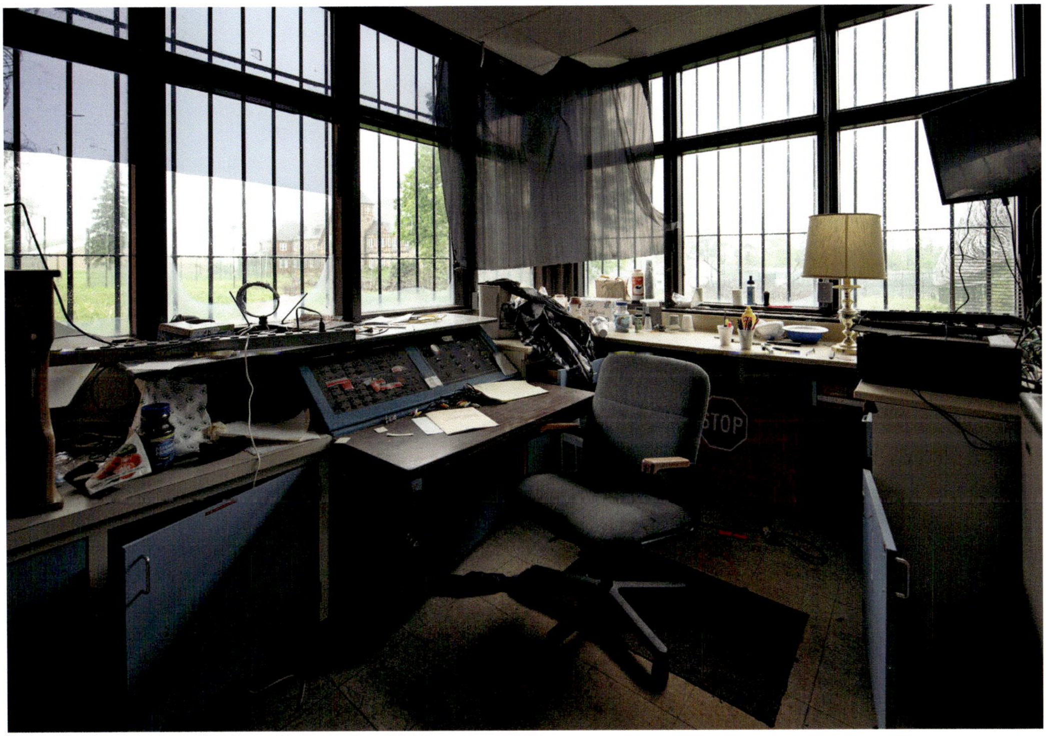

Much was left behind in the main guards' office.

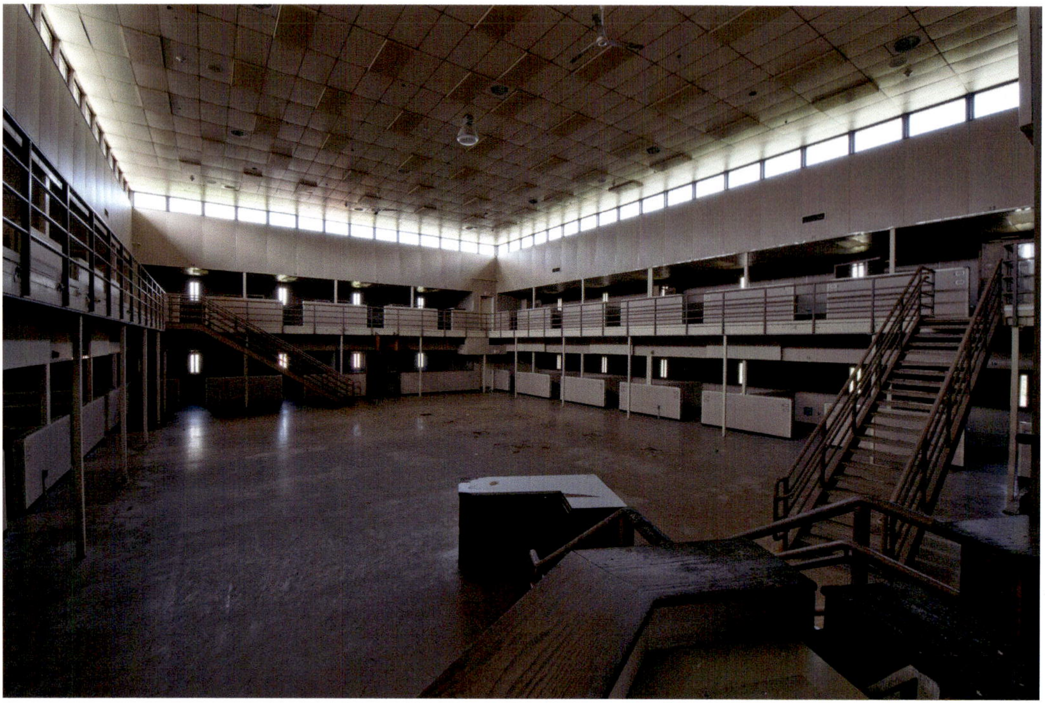

This building, now off limits, had a much different color scheme than the other housing units. I believe this was for juveniles, as there were no cell doors.

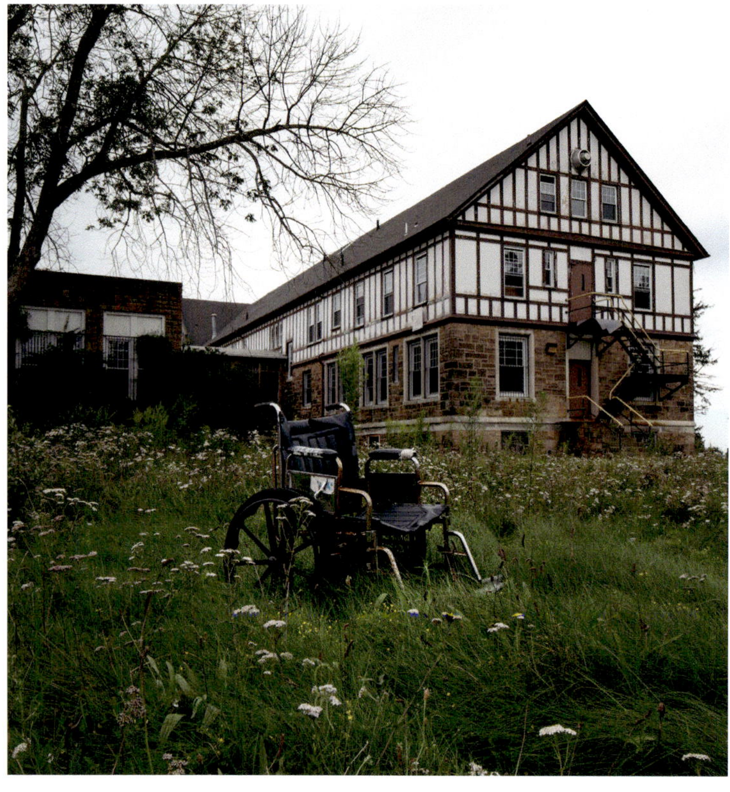

An old wheelchair sits in an overgrown courtyard by the medical building.

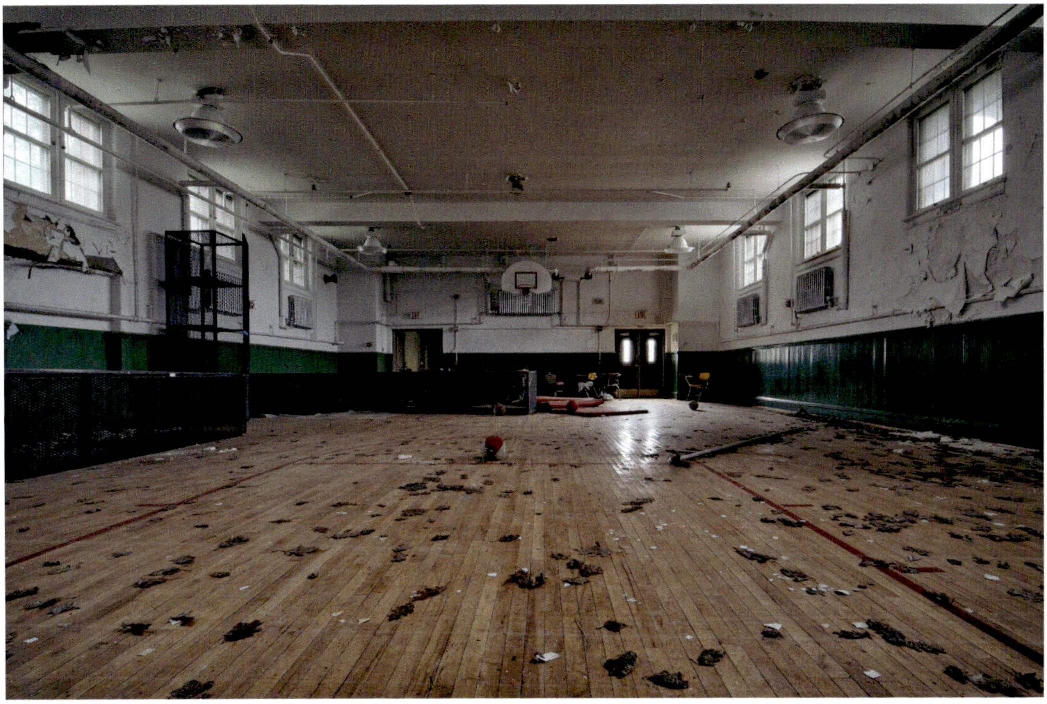

A gym in the basement of the Administrative Building.

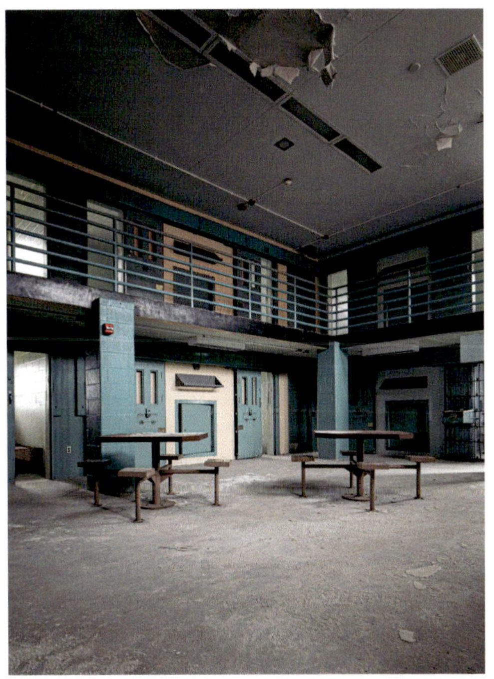

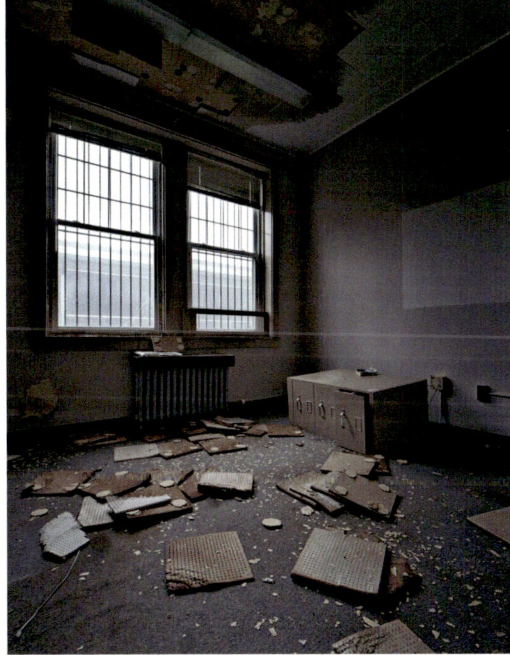

Above left: The cell block in the mental health unit in the prison.

Above right: Ceiling tiles litter the floor of what was once an office in the Medical Inmate Services Building.

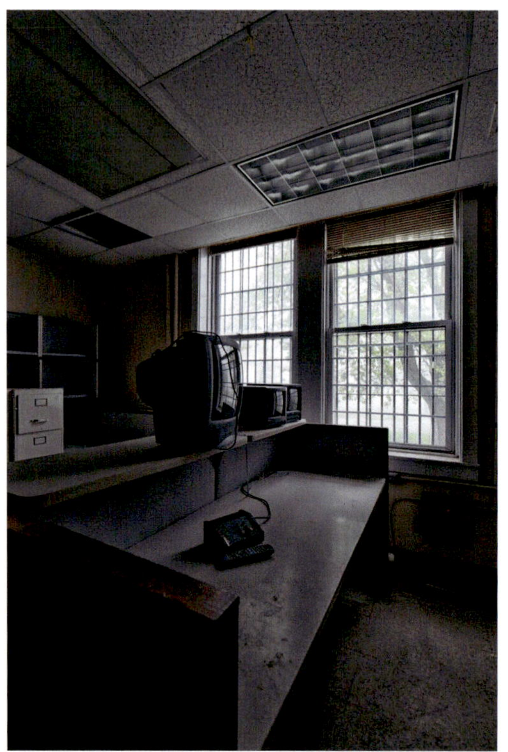

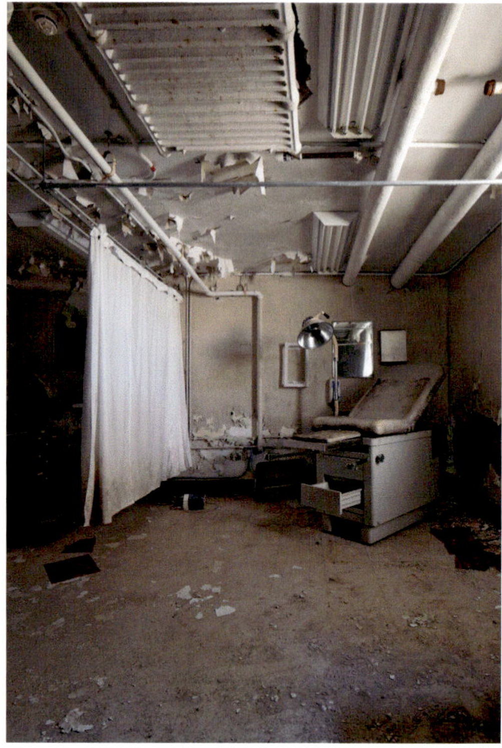

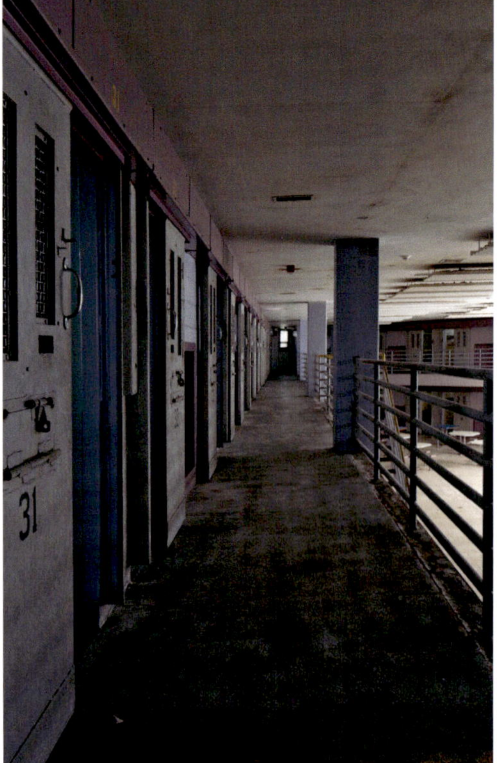

Above left: TVs sit in a guard office in the administrative building.

Above right: An old exam chair in the basement of the medical building, still with the curtain drawn.

Left: The upper level of one of the cell blocks.

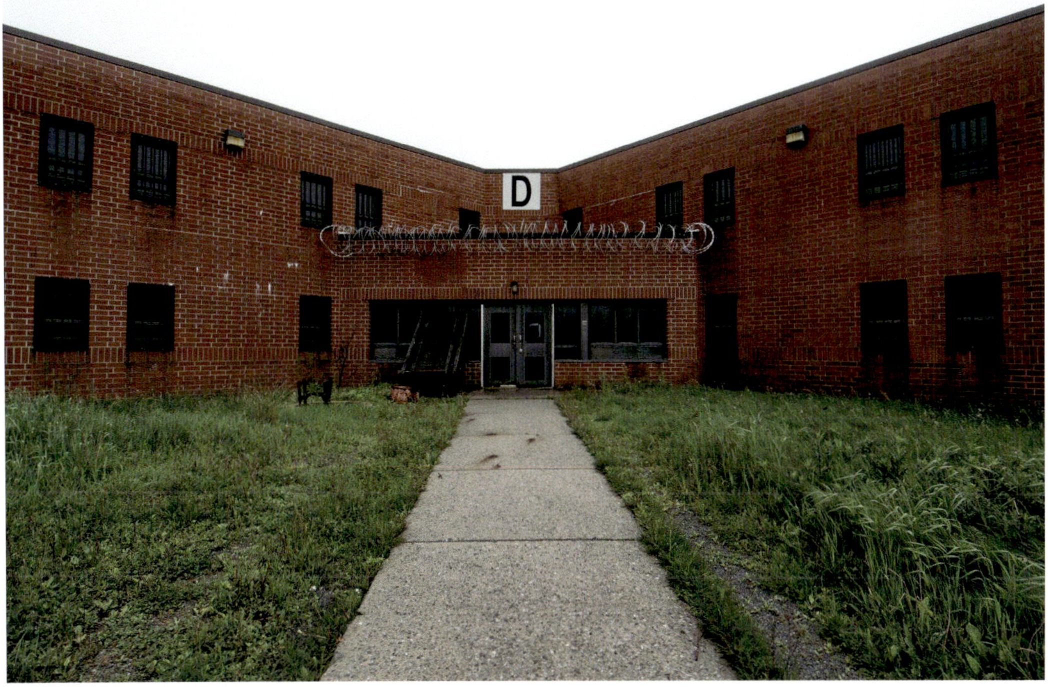

Housing Unit D.

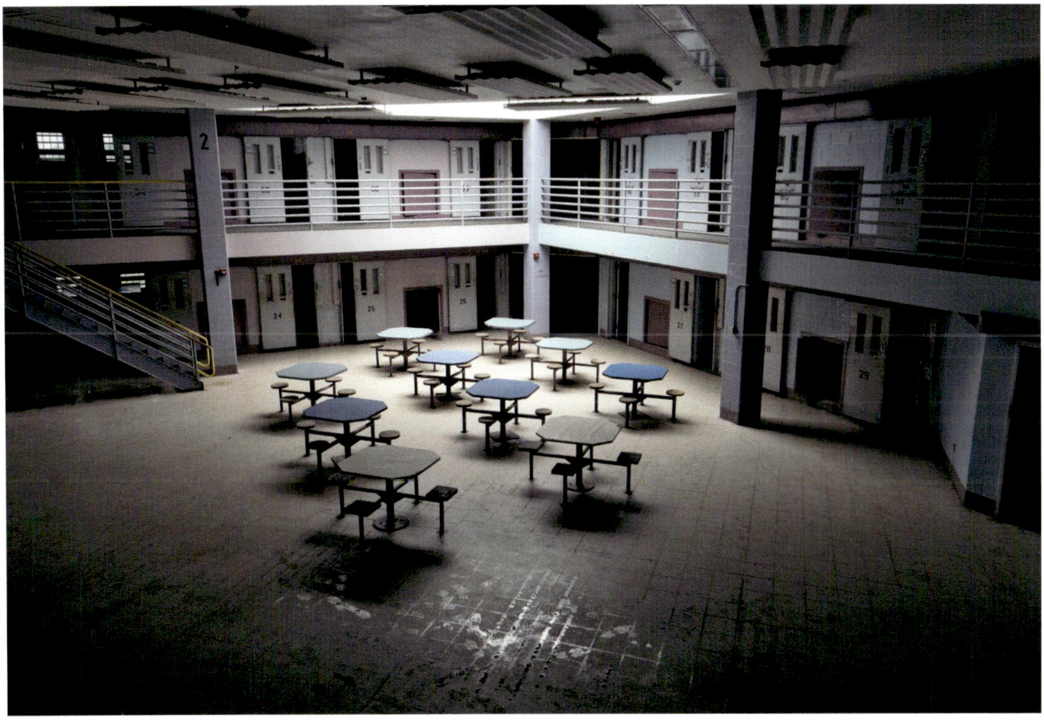

A view of the common area in the cell block. The calm, quiet stillness felt displaced.

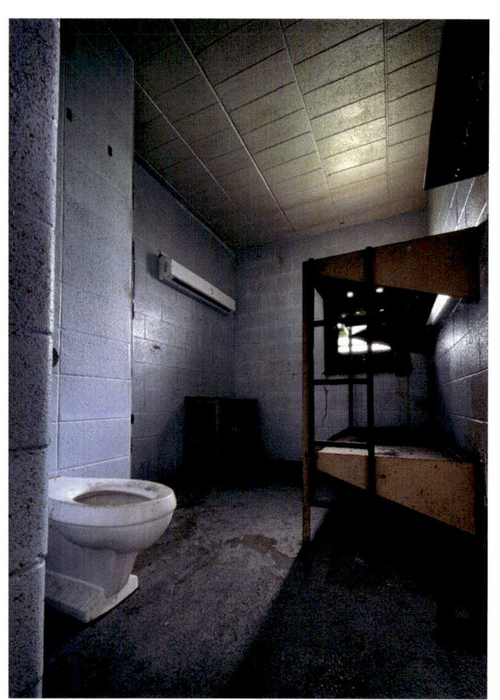

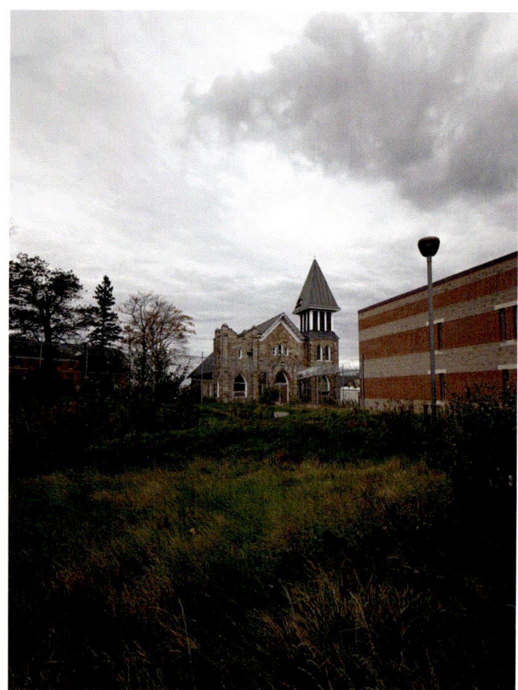

Above left: A view of an empty cell.

Above right: The chapel sits in the middle of the property, crowded by two housing units.

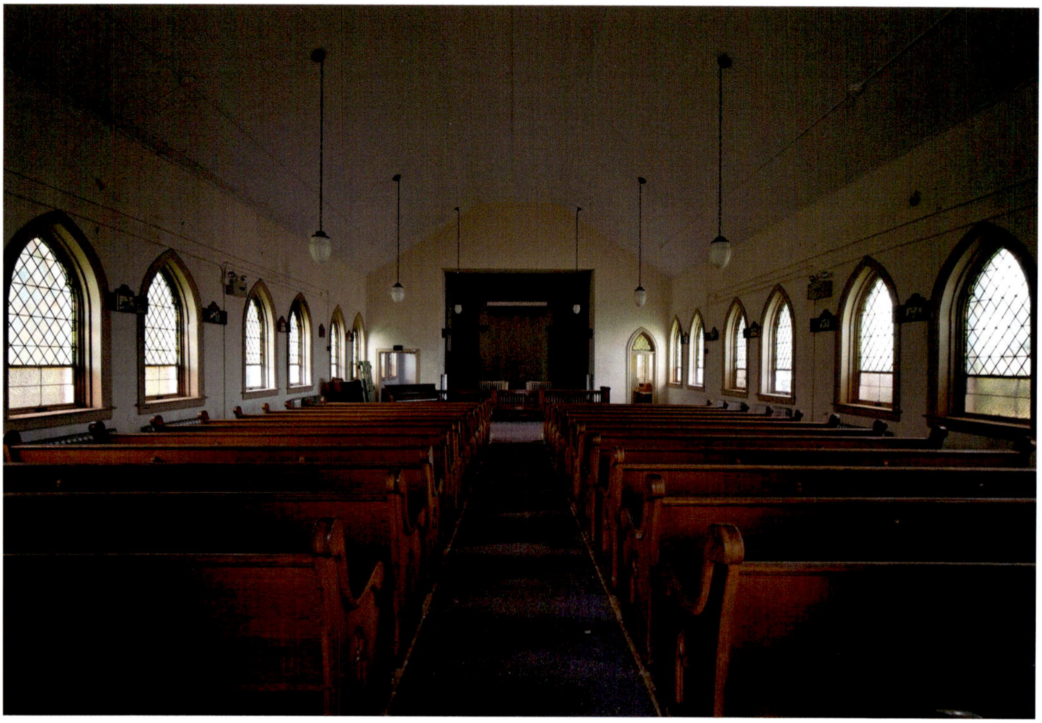

Grace Chapel.

15

TROLLEY GRAVEYARD

Hidden away in a small town in Western Pennsylvania sits nearly four dozen streetcars collected from cities like Chicago, Boston, Pittsburgh, Philadelphia, and Cleveland. Spread out over around 20 acres; these trolley cars sit decaying in hopes of being saved. President of the Vintage Electric Streetcar Company and owner of the trolleys, Ed Metka, provides parts to help those who cannot find parts to make repairs due to these streetcars no longer being manufactured. The Massachusetts Bay Transportation Authority (MBTA) still uses these streetcars in Boston. Berwin Coal once used the buildings on the property to repair and build coal cars. It comes as no surprise to find some of the trolley cars have been located on the property since the 1990s. They are heavily covered in graffiti, leaves, and debris from fallen roofs. Even with graffiti, it is not hard to imagine how magnificent the trolleys once were. The owner was kind enough to show me some of the trolleys stored safely from the elements and untouched by vandals.

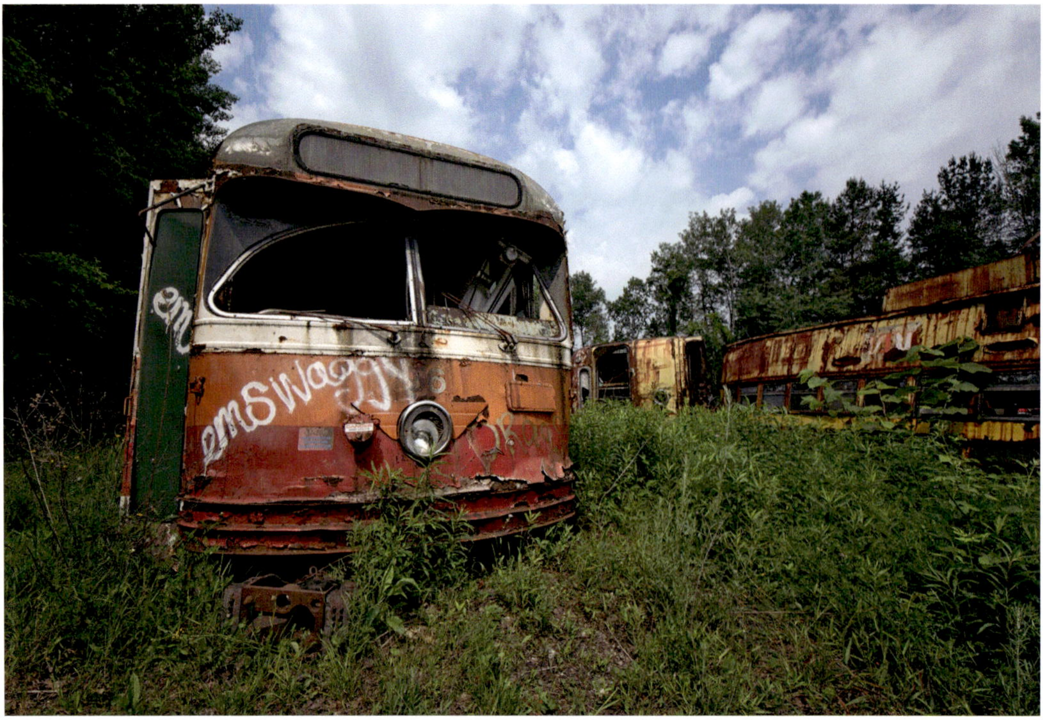

An old trolley car sits alone with two others in the front of the property.

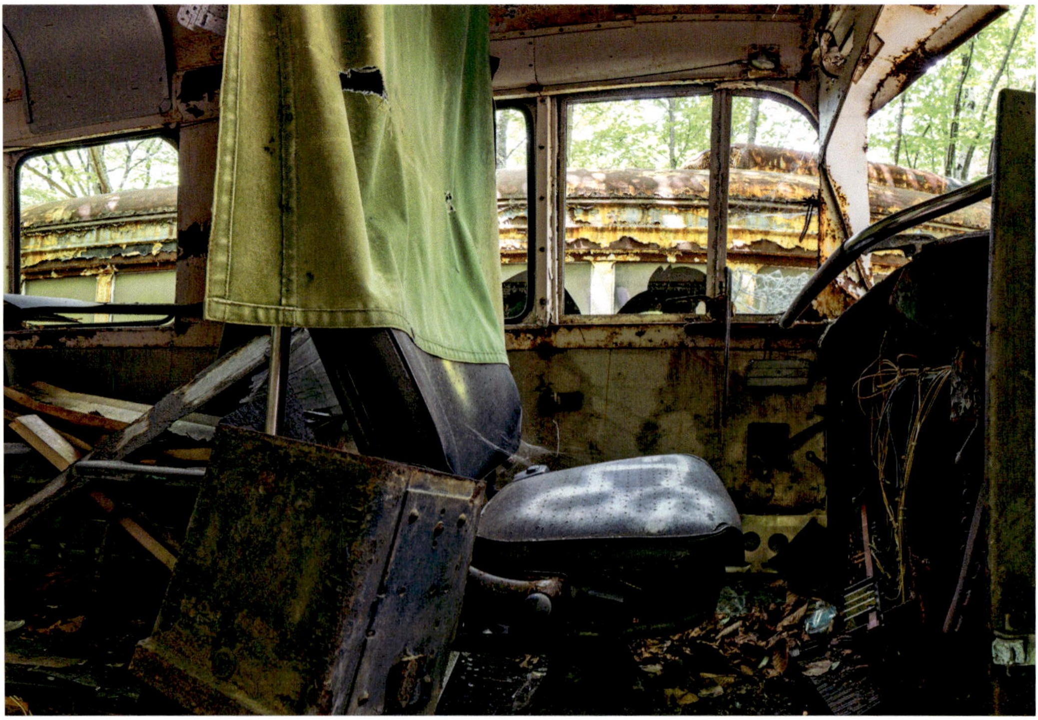

The front seat of the trolley.

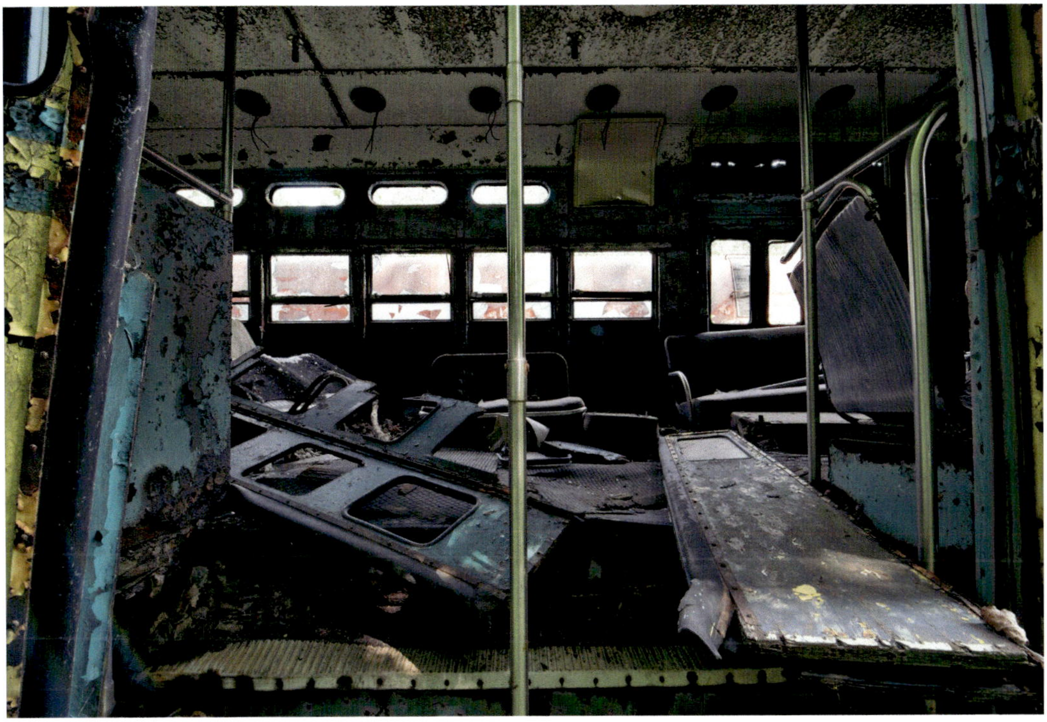

The old doors have rusted off and collapsed inside. It was interesting how the metal handles remained shiny with no corrosion.

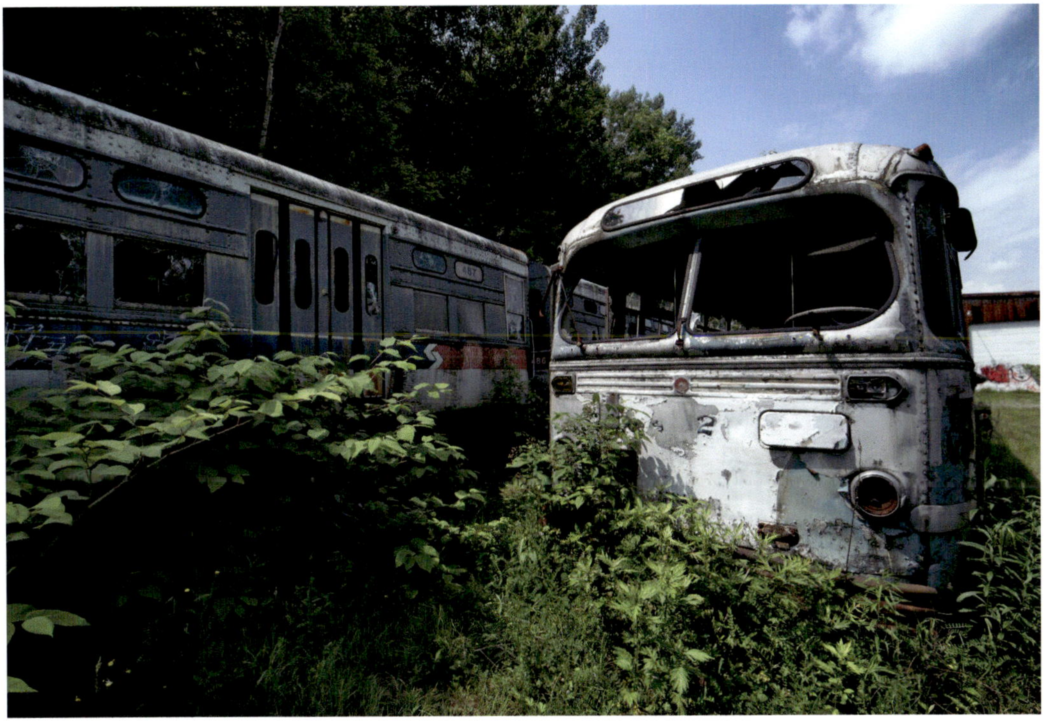

An old bus sits next to a series of trolley cars.

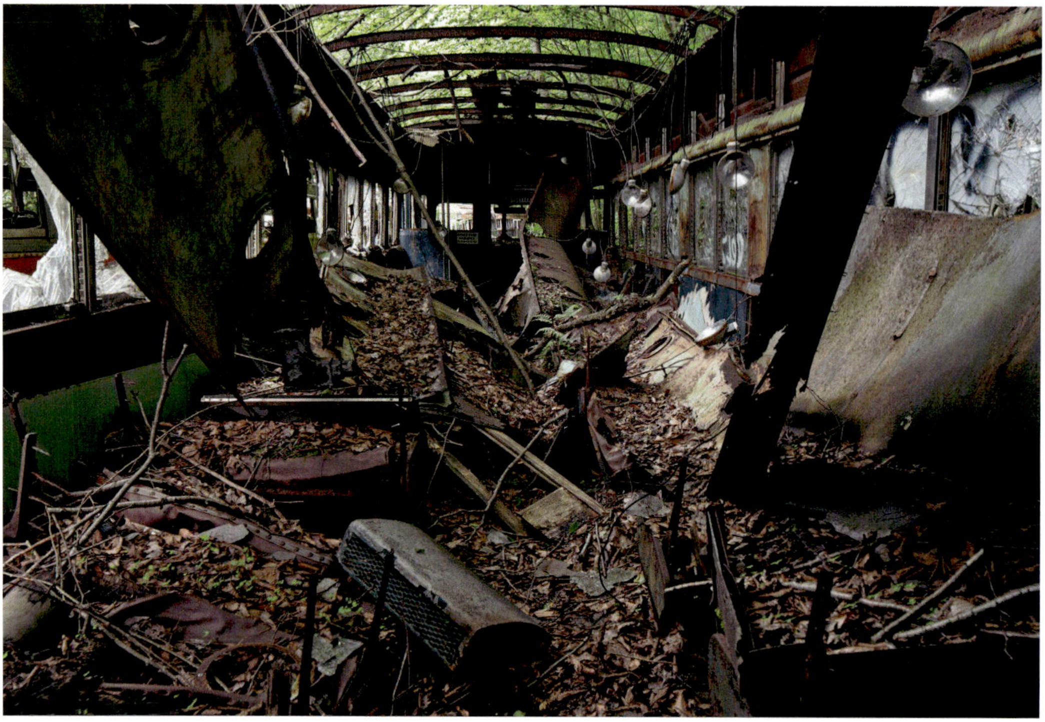

The roof completely rusted out and collapsed into the trolley car.

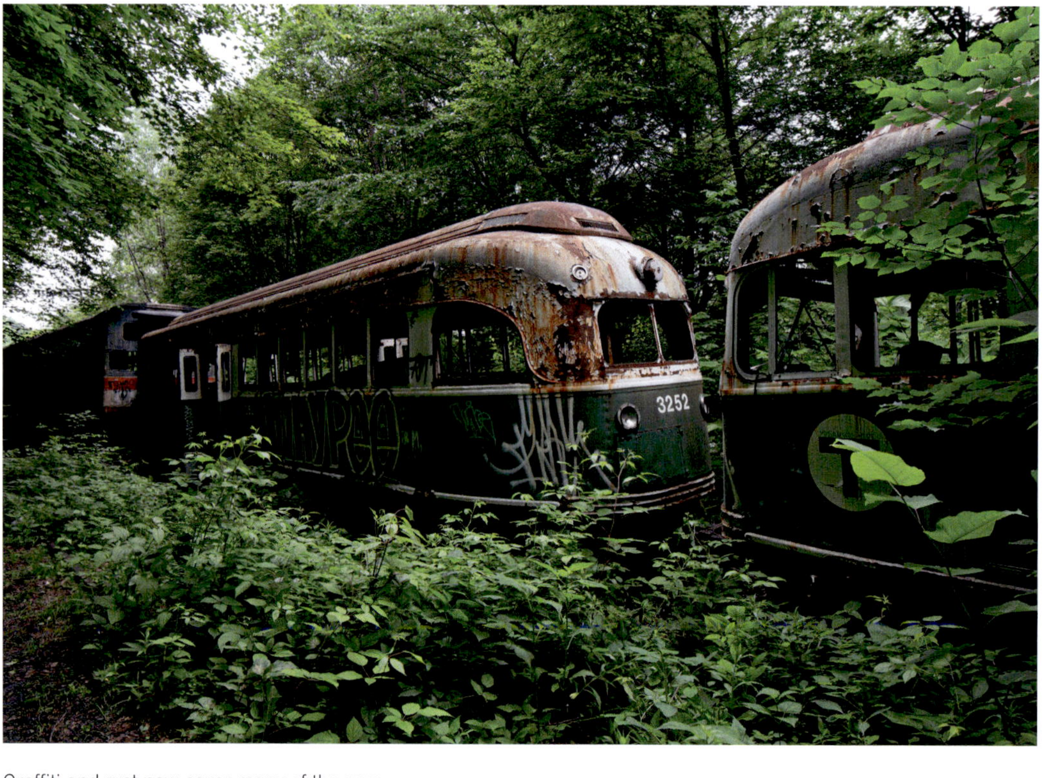

Graffiti and rust now cover many of the cars.

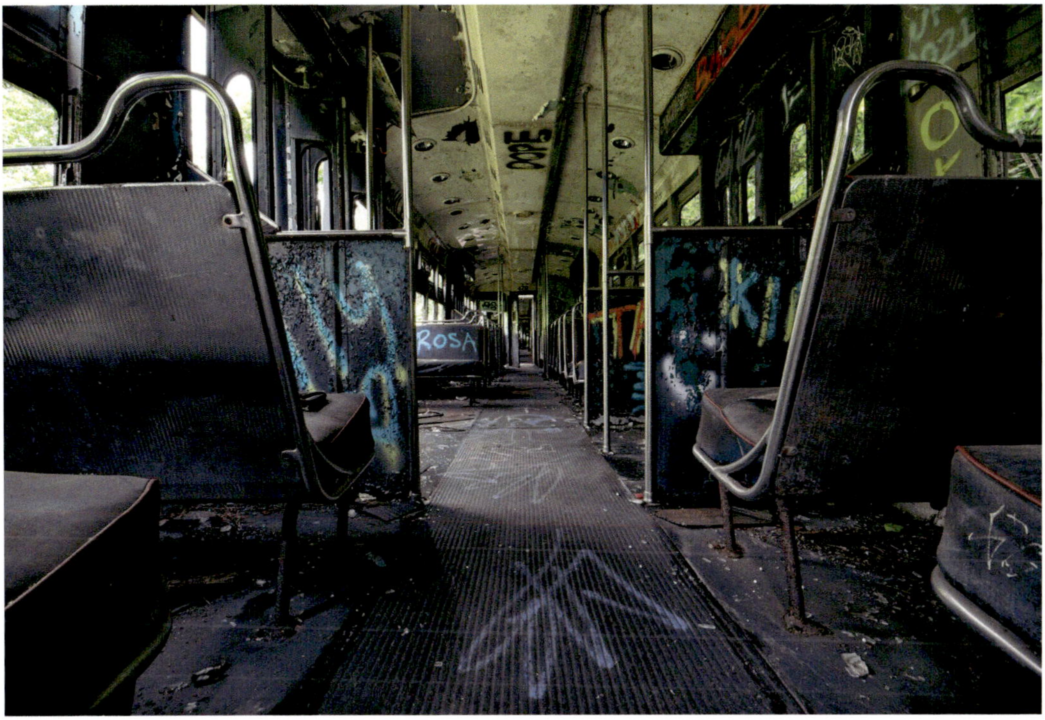

It felt like the trolley cars were never-ending.

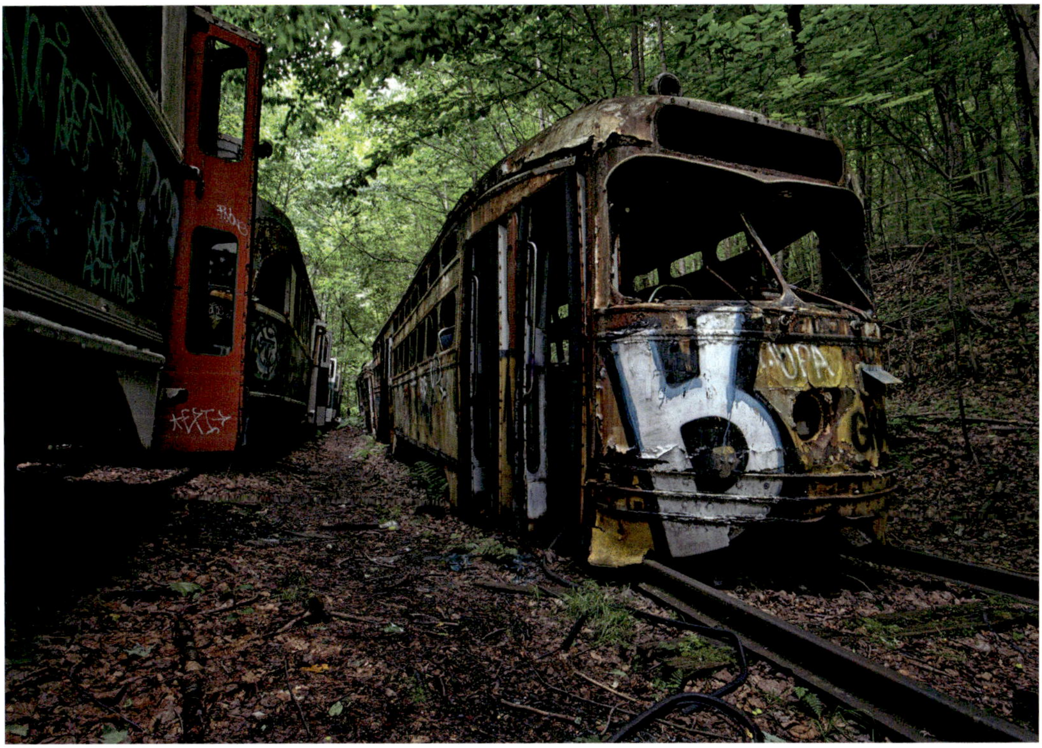

Forever frozen on the tracks.

16

UNION STATION BUILDING

Located on Market Street in Brownsville, Pennsylvania, the Union Station building was built between 1927 and 1928 by the Monongahela Railway Company. This building replaced a smaller station that was built in the 1800s. The five-story high building was made of brick, granite, and marble with twenty bay windows and a curved façade. Every twenty minutes, a passenger train would leave the station. By 1915, the Union Station had sixty-eight passenger trains daily. In 1920, the passenger service on the Dunlap Creek Division was discontinued. This meant only four trains made their way through Brownsville a day. Until 1993, the building contained railroad offices and privately owned businesses. The last business moved out in 2000 after the heat was cut off from the building. Today, the property sits empty, with no light at the end of the tunnel.

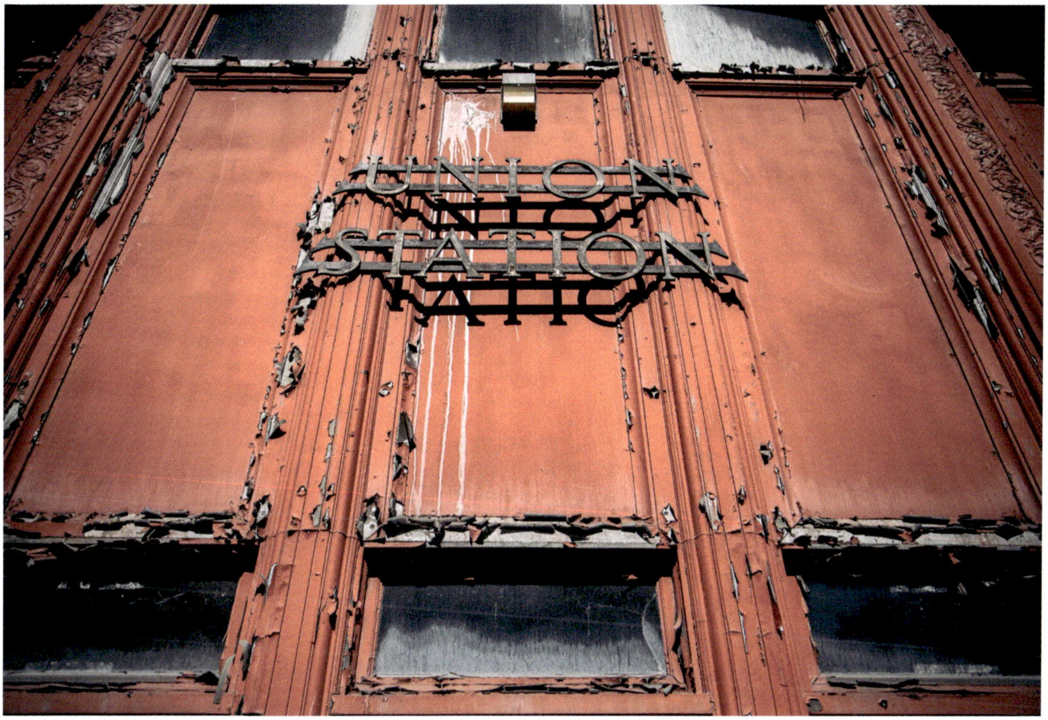

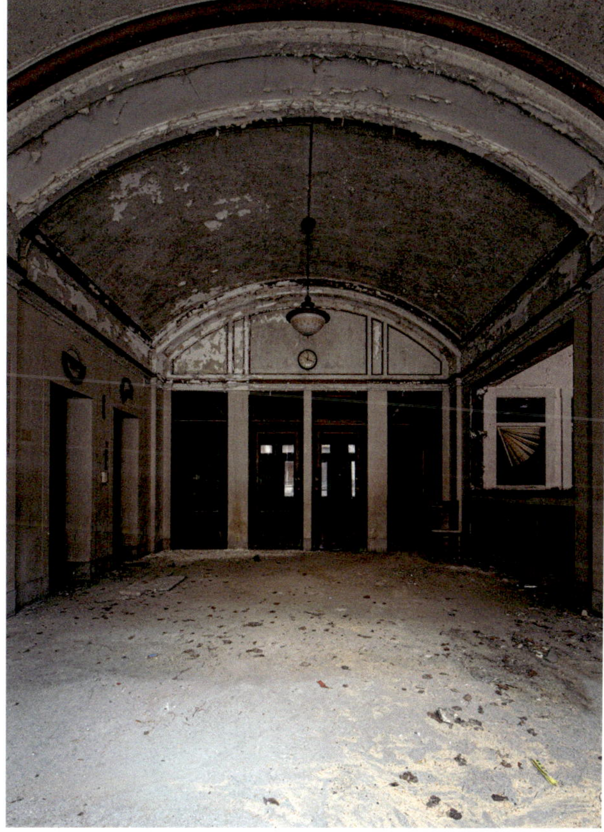

Above: The old Union Station sign still sits proudly above the main doors to the train station.

Right: The main lobby of the station.

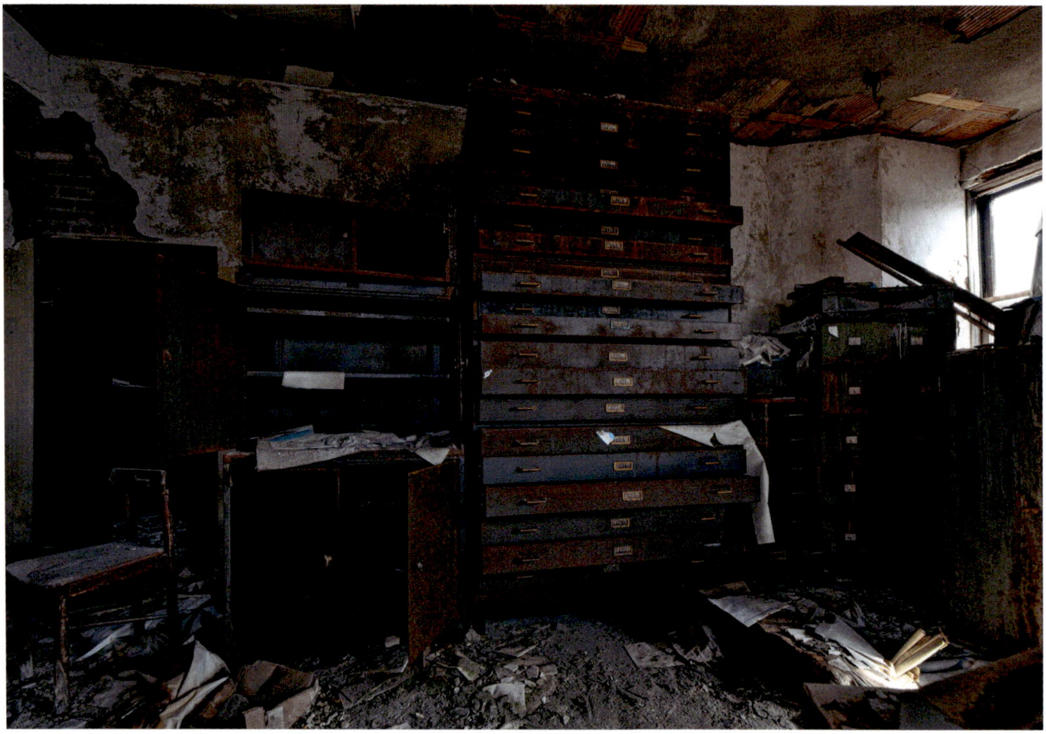

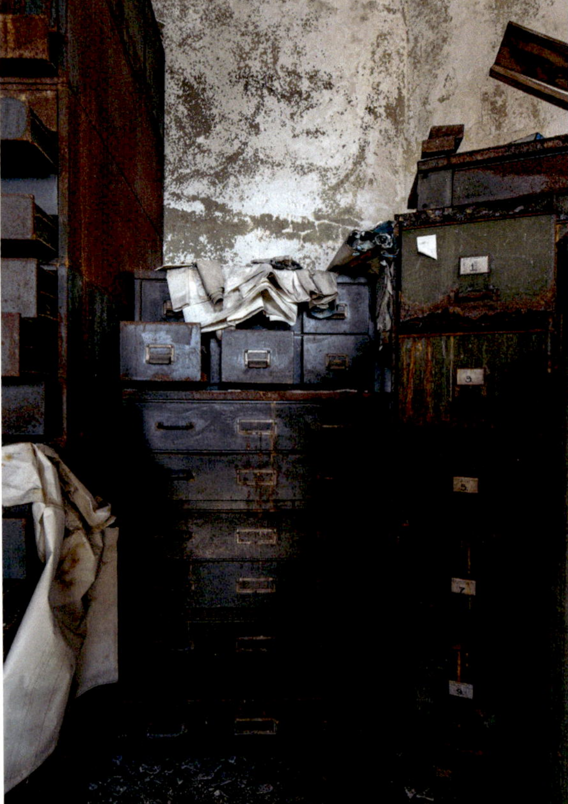

Above: Blueprint cabinets still contain the blueprints for the old trains.

Left: Many of the doors had rusted shut.

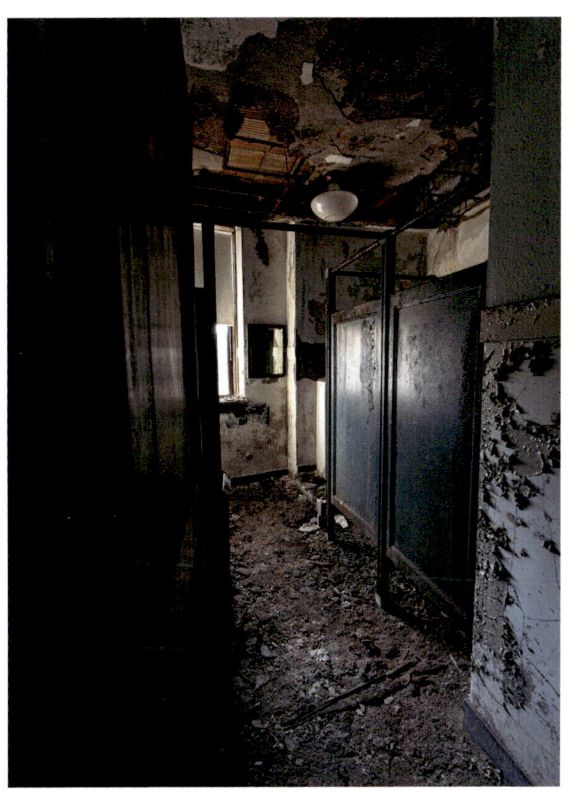

The ceiling of one of the restrooms begins to chip away, exposing brick.

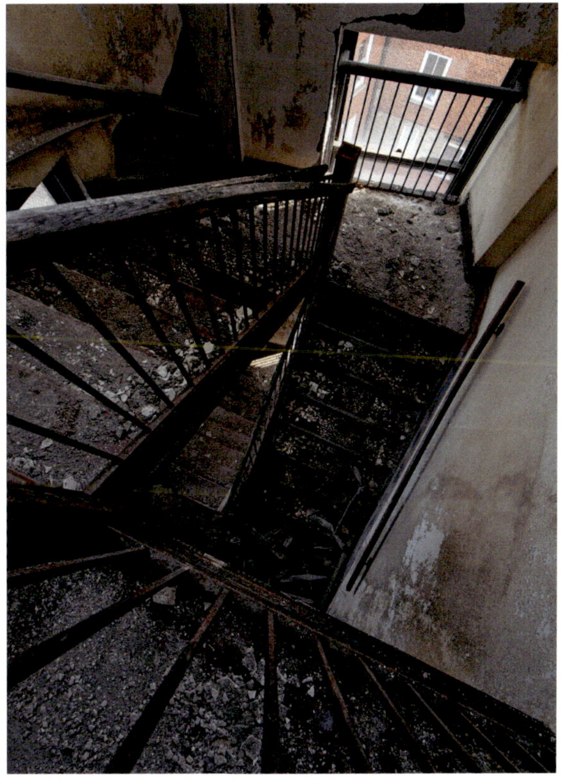

A long winding staircase. This one led straight into the basement.

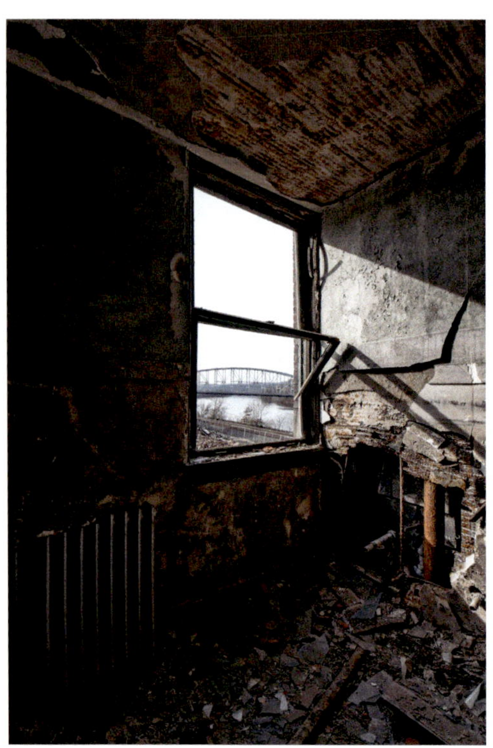

Left: The Brownsville bridge can be seen from the windows of the old station. Scrappers have removed what might have been copper piping from this room.

Below: Light from the distant staircase offered a glimpse of the elevators.

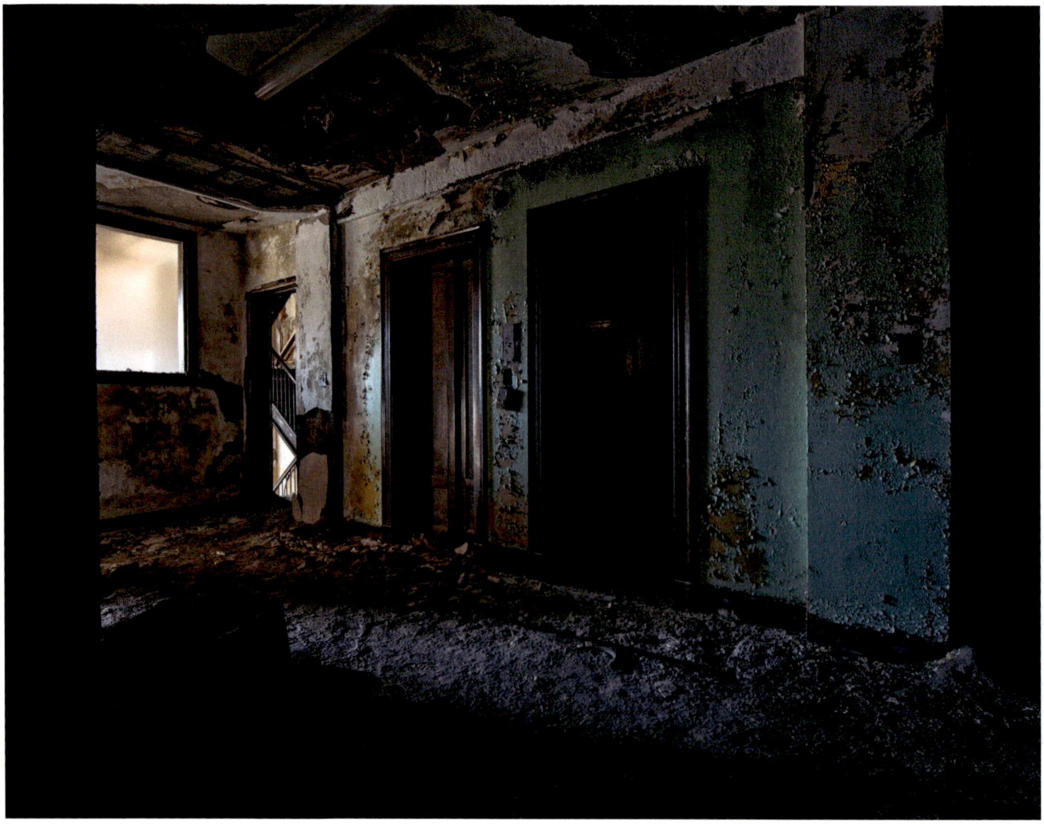

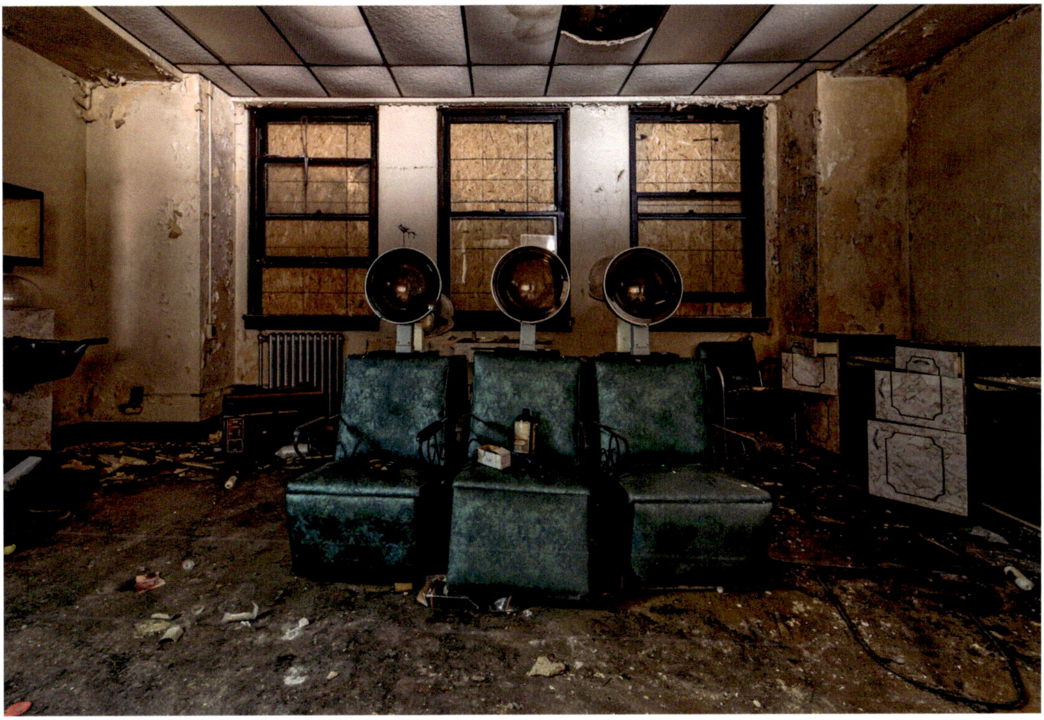

Hooded dryer chairs were left in what was once a hair salon in the station.

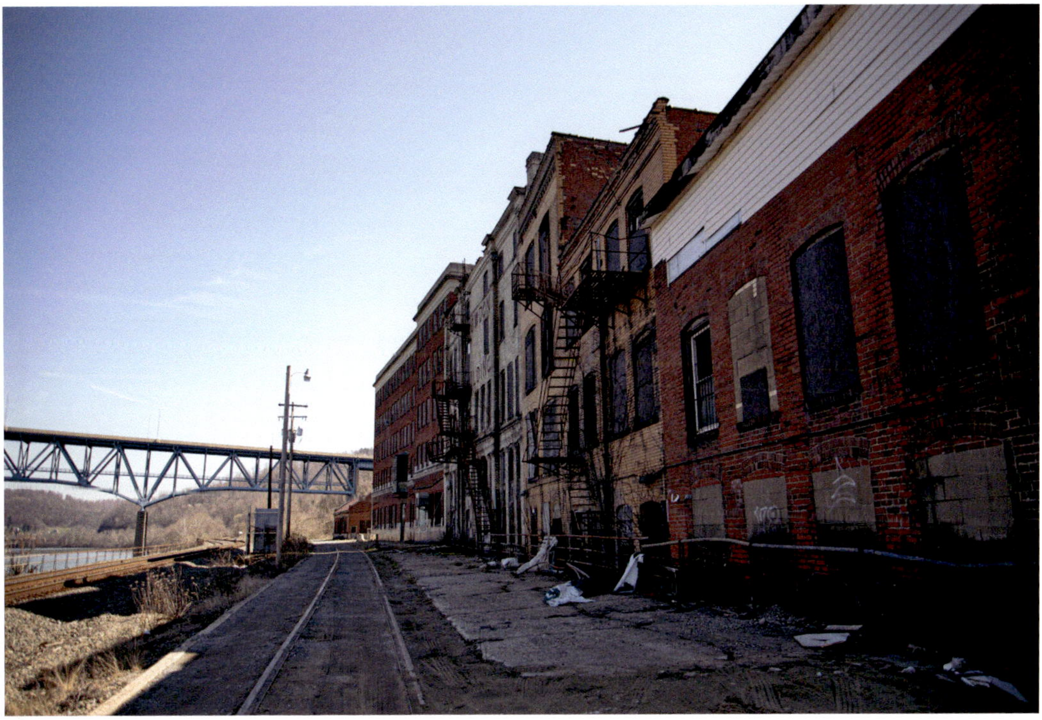

A view from the tracks. The Union Station can be seen all the way at the end on the right. The other buildings in this photo have been torn down.

17

WELLS VALLEY CHAPEL

Hidden in the outskirts of Hagerstown is the long-abandoned Wells Valley Chapel. The church was erected in 1853. The attached cemetery is known as the Roaring Run Cemetery.

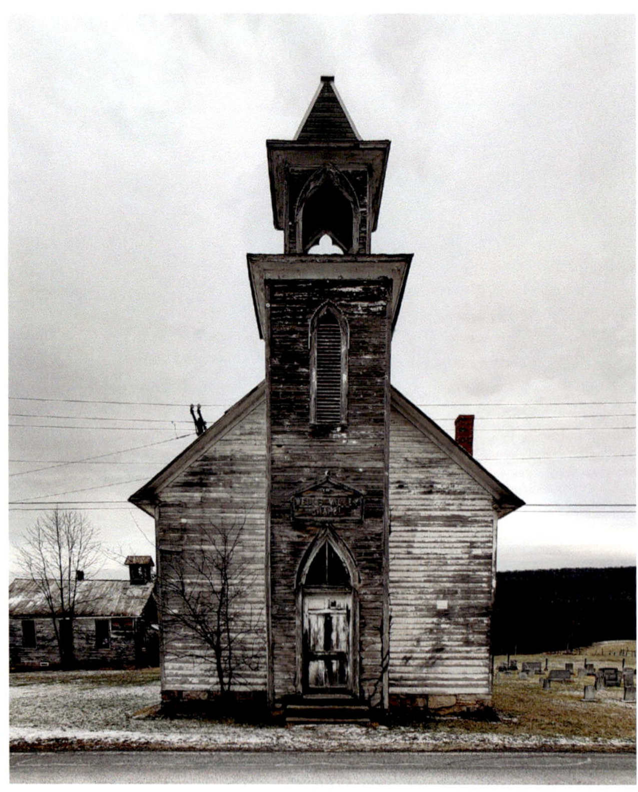

The church is wholly gutted today.

18

WESTINGHOUSE ATOM SMASHER

Hidden in the suburbs of Pittsburgh, the Westinghouse Atom Smasher was a 5-MeV (Maximal extractable value) Van de Graaff electrostatic nuclear accelerator. Today, atom smashers are known as particle accelerators. The Westinghouse Atom Smasher was in use from 1937 until 1958. The accelerator utilized two high-speed belts that carried electric charges to a mushroom-shaped electrode at the tip of the bulb-shaped enclosure. Ions such as helium gas or hydrogen gas were injected into the accelerator tube, causing an electrostatic potential between the bottom and top of the tube, causing subatomic particles to reach high velocities of speed as they traveled through the cylinder. These particles were guided to hit targeted atoms, smashing them to create nuclear energy. The smasher sat unused from 1958 until the property was purchased in 2012 with the intent to build apartments in place of the facility. In 2013, there were talks of the local school district using the smasher as a centerpiece for an educational facility they hoped to build. However, that project never came to fruition. As you can imagine, by 2015, the property was heavily decayed and vandalized. In January 2015, the smasher was laid on its side after being removed from its support stand.

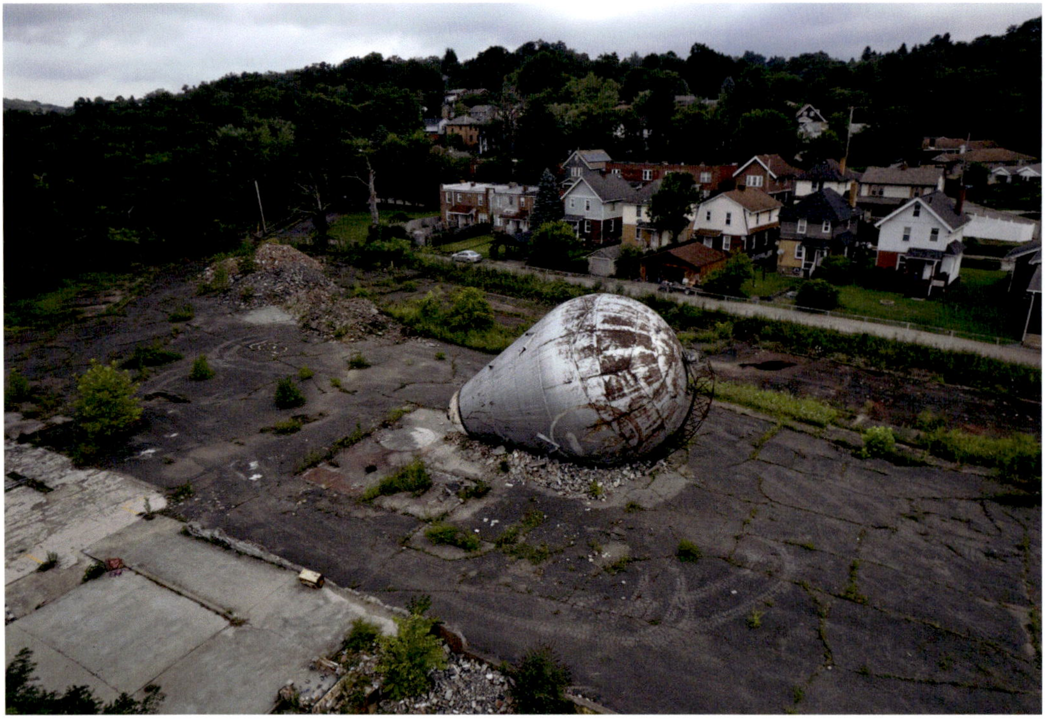

A bird's eye view of the atom smasher shows how big it really is compared to the homes beside it.

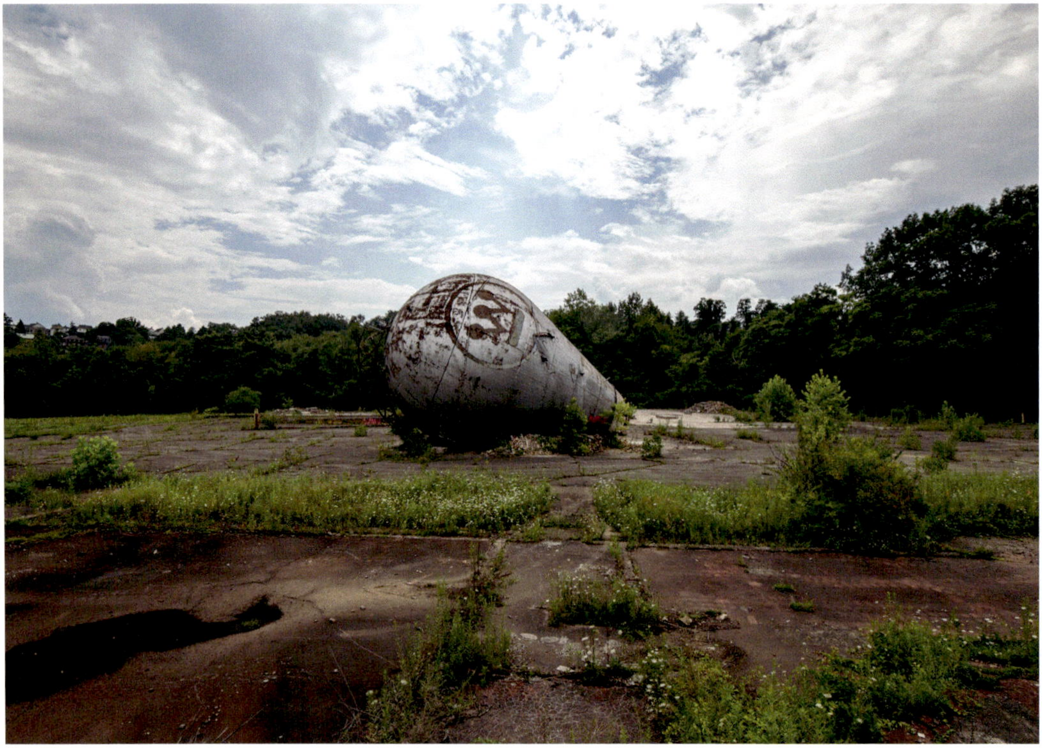

There is a small hangout spot hidden behind the smasher, unable to be seen from the road.

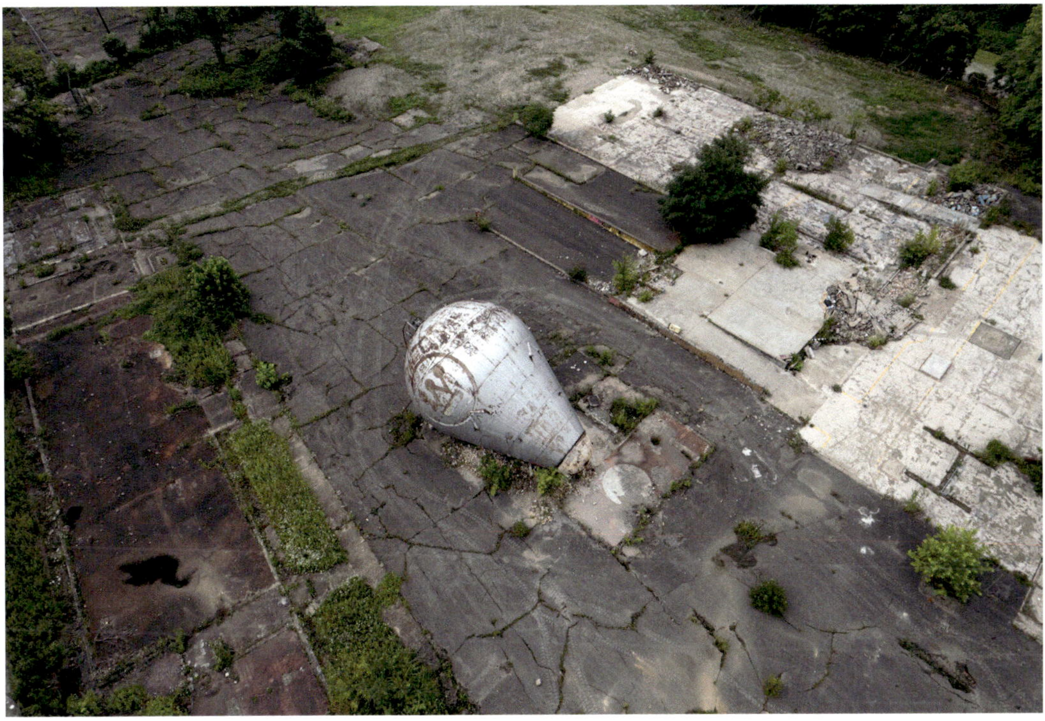

You can see the foundation of where the old building used to sit.

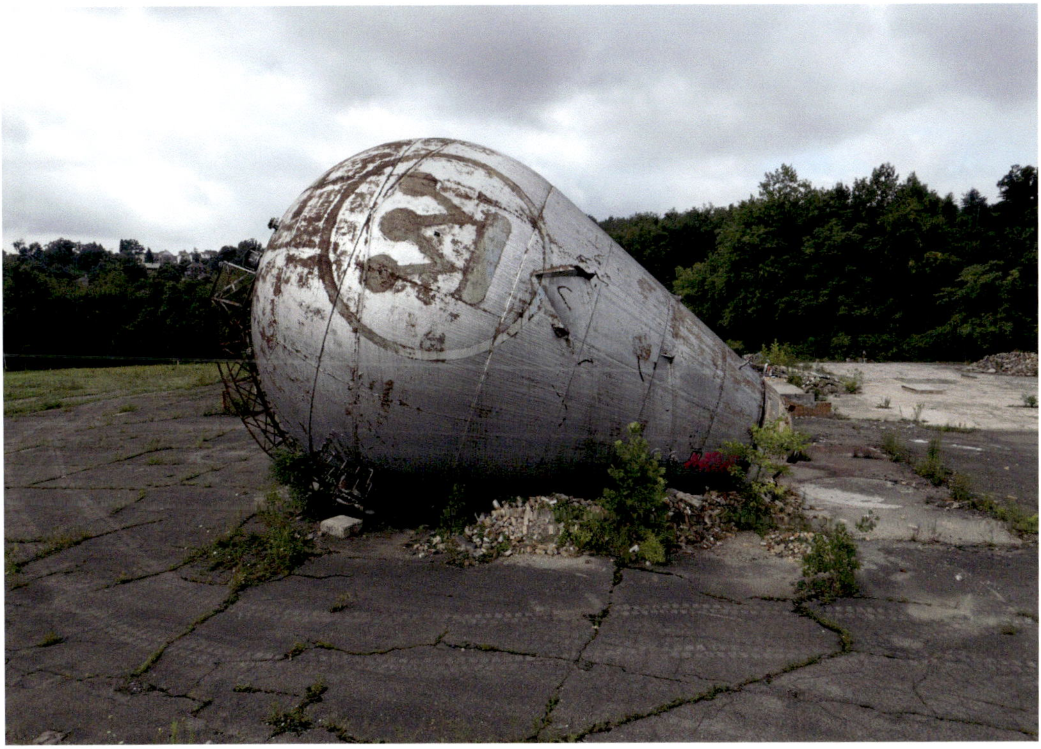

Today, the smasher sits tipped on its side, waiting to be refurbished and restored to its iconic glory.

19

YELLOW DOG VILLAGE

Located west of Kittanning in Worthington, Pennsylvania, is an abandoned village known as Yellow Dog. The village was built for the workers of the nearby mines and factories. Pittsburgh Limestone Company-owned limestone mines spanned out over 150 miles. In the early 1900s, it was not easy to travel. Pittsburgh Limestone Company built a community near the mines for their workers to improve productivity. The company made a contract with the workers that they would raise wages if they agreed not to form a union. This kind of contract is called a yellow dog contract, hence the name Yellow Dog Village.

The village was built between the years 1910 and 1920. The village comprises nineteen homes, a boarding house, and a large manager's house. The limestone mines shut down in the 1950s, leading to the end of Yellow Dog Village. A well contamination was the next hit the village took. Then the housing crisis in the early 2000s. The last family left the village in 2010. From 2010 until 2014, the village sat abandoned. In 2014, Joe Meyer purchased the property to restore the homes and open the village back up as a time capsule. The thought was that visitors would stay in period housing. They would spend their time there without modern convenience for a week or weekend. And learn skills to survive without electricity, running water, or heat. Since 2017, there has not been much noise from the owner or renovation happening.

I have visited the village a few times in the last few years. Sadly, the plan to save the village looks grim. Many of the structurally sound homes are falling into disrepair.

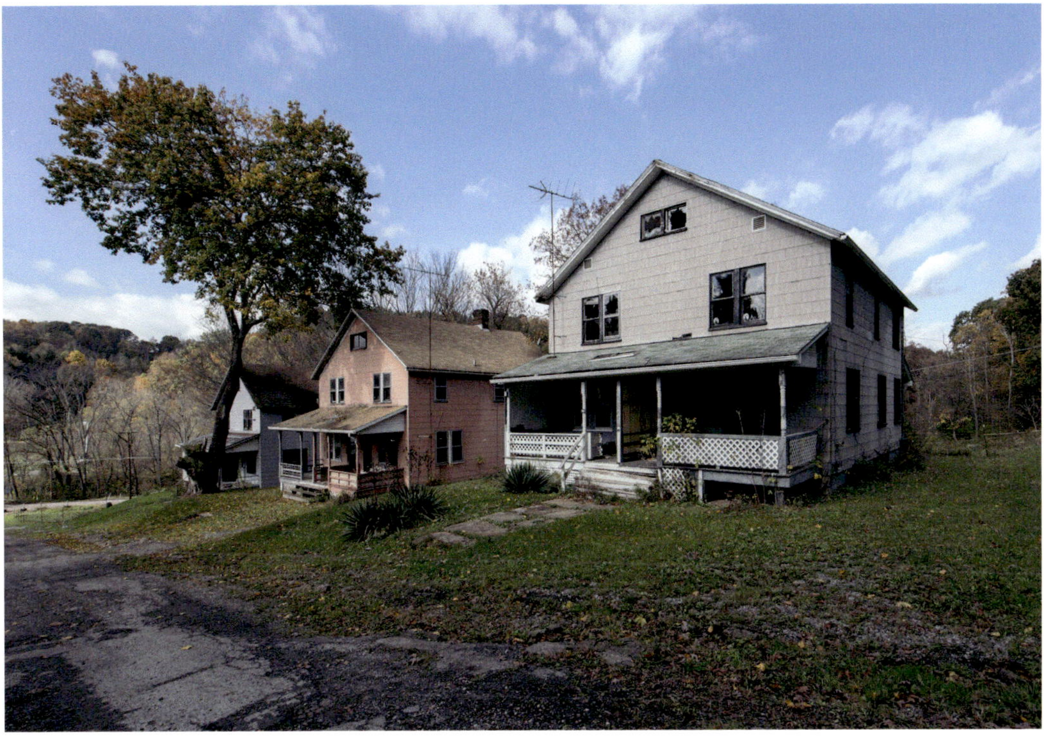

These three houses are close to the main road and sit on the edge of the property.

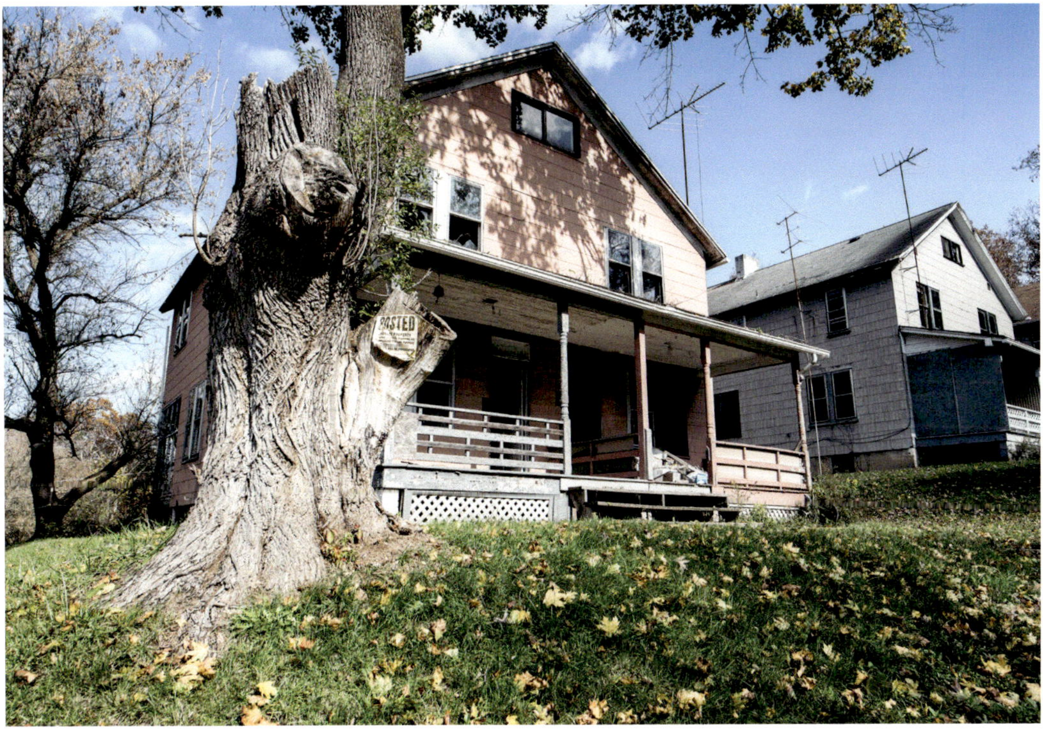

A posted sign fades as the house decays.

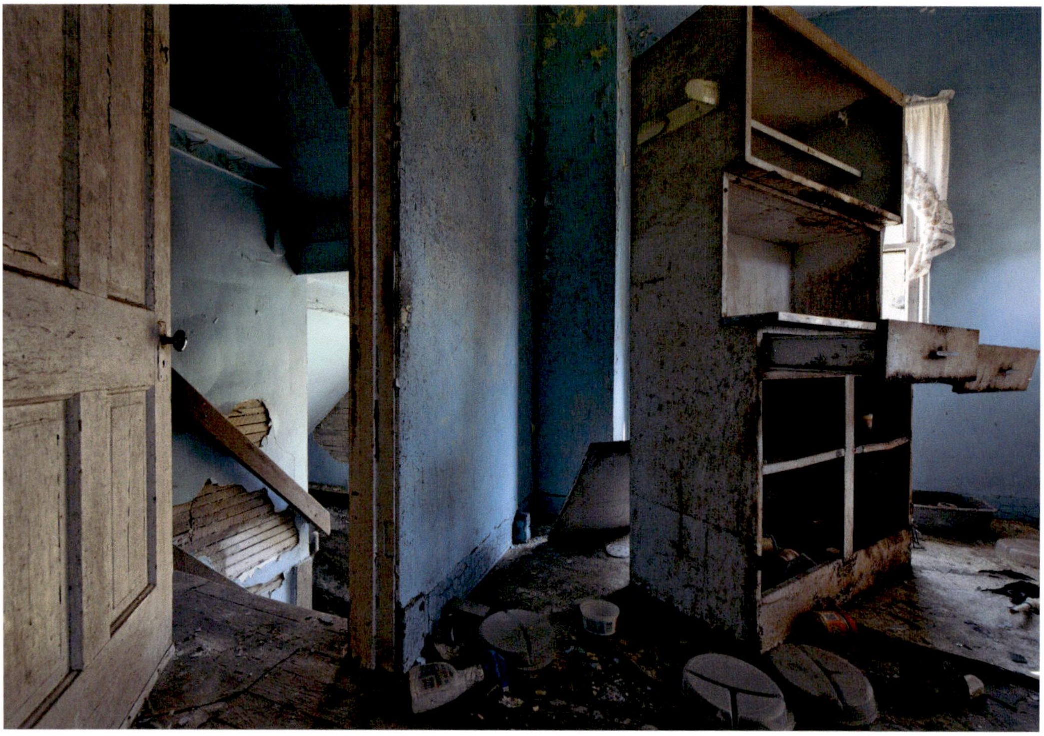

Many of the homes were still mostly furbished.

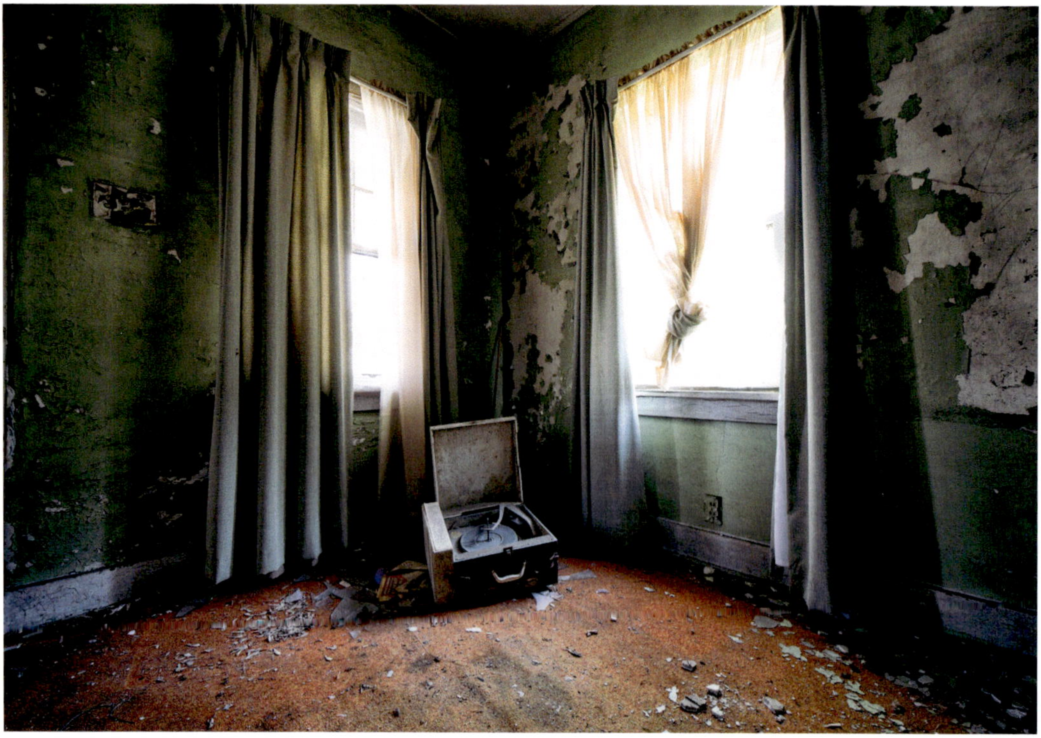

An old record player begins to mold and rust in the living room.

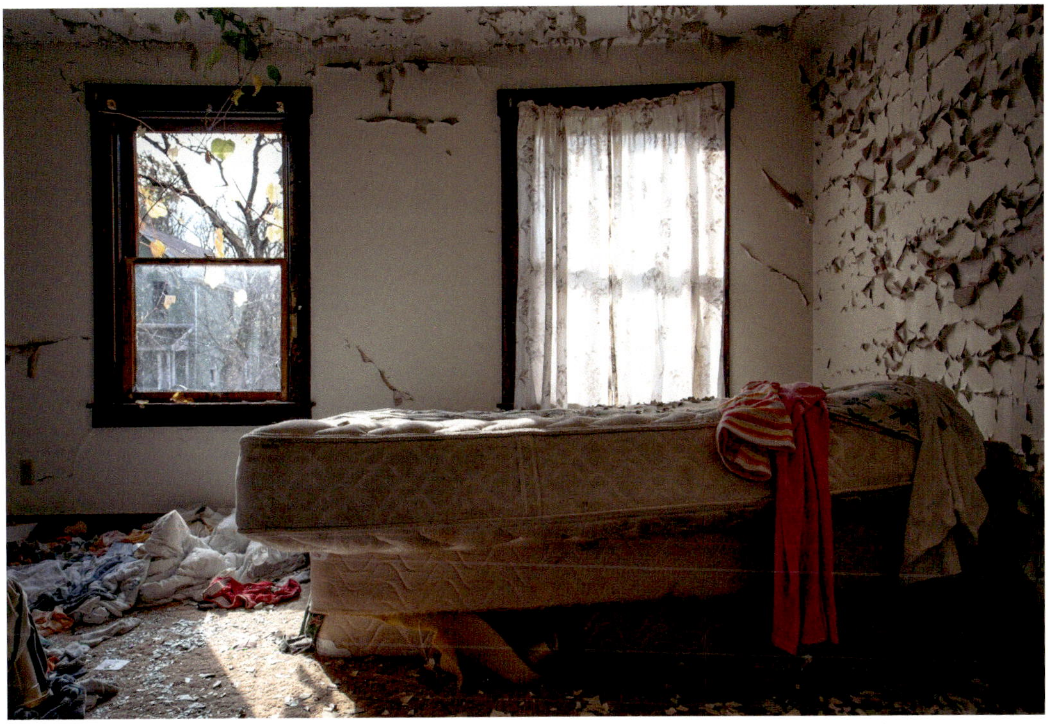

Branches of a nearby tree growing through a broken window in an upstairs bedroom.

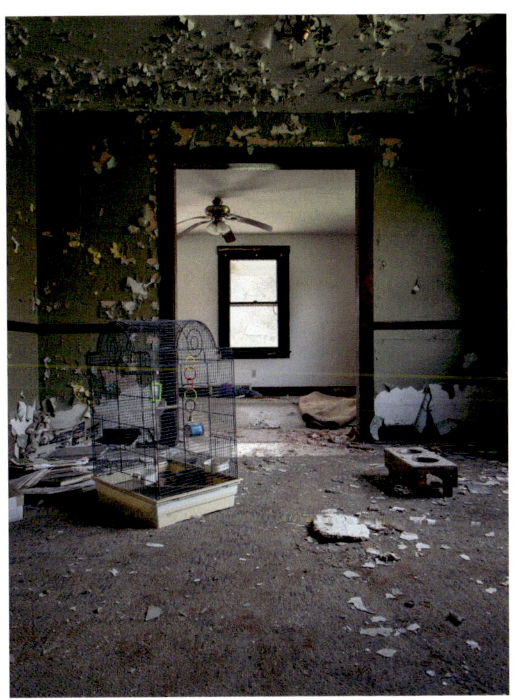

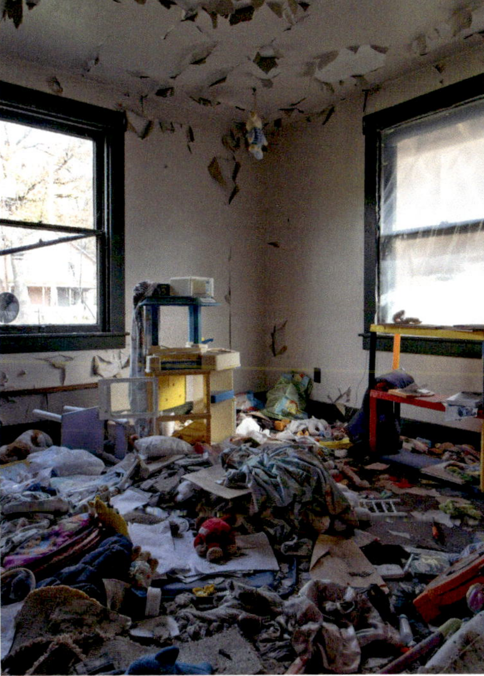

Above left: A birdcage and feeding bowl holder leave clues suggesting the owners must have had pets.

Above right: An eerie sight of a teddy bear hung from the ceiling in what appears to have been a child's room.

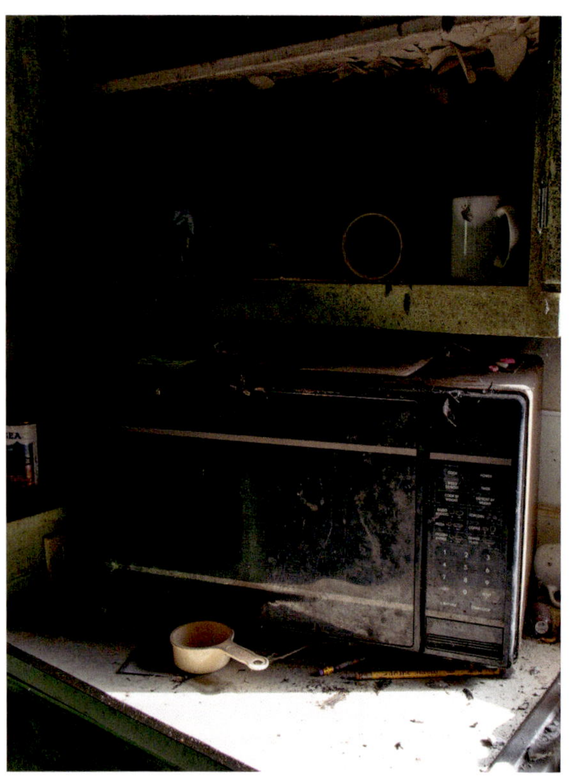

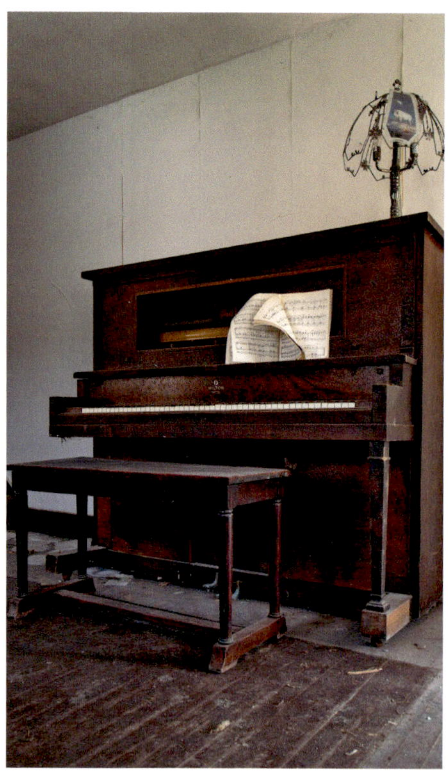

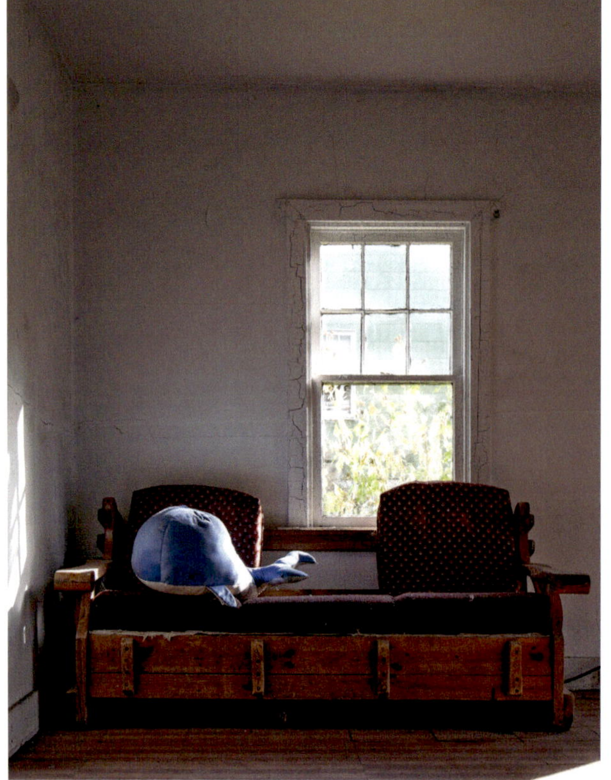

Above left: Dishes were left in the cabinets and sinks. Appliances remained plugged in, waiting to be used.

Above right: I was surprised to find a working piano in one of the homes. Sheet music still rested on the upper panel.

Left: A lonely stuffed whale sits on a couch in one of the empty homes.

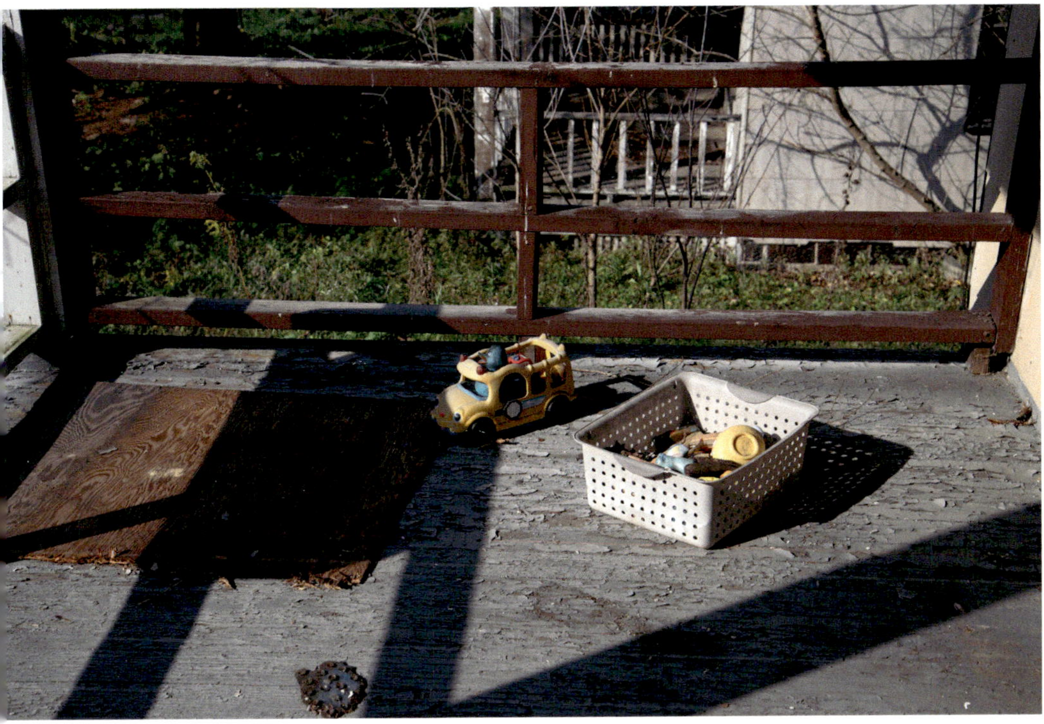

Children's toys left behind on the porch of one of the homes.

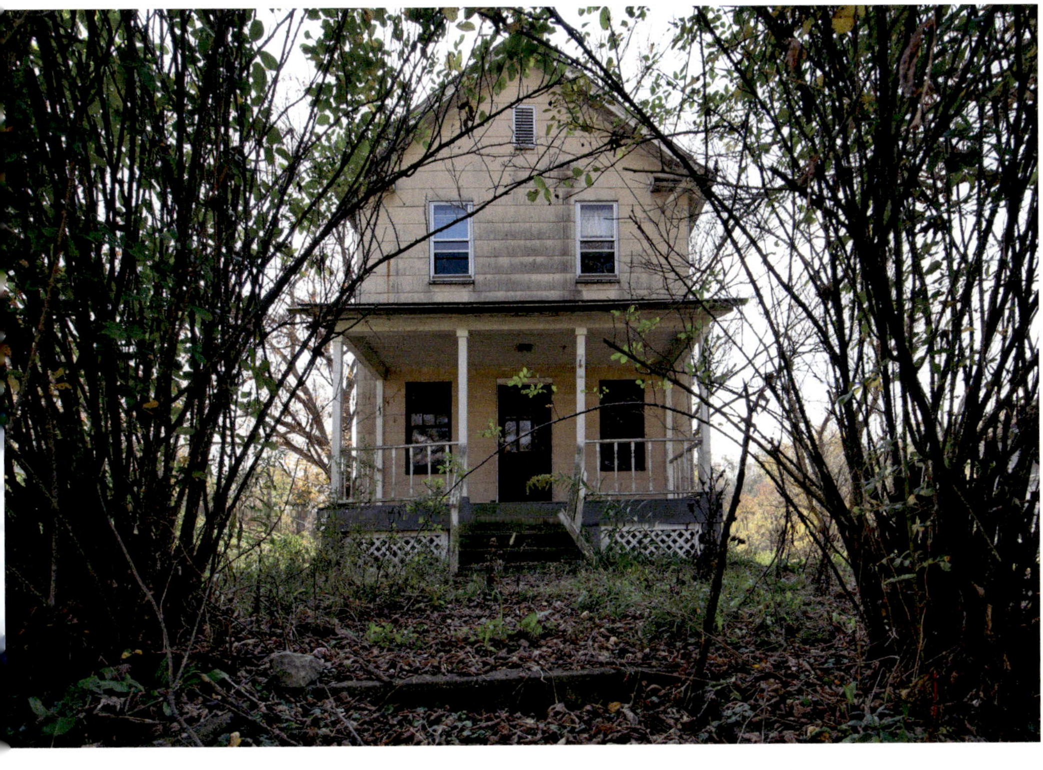

Foliage has grown to cover the sidewalk; with enough time, the house will be hidden.

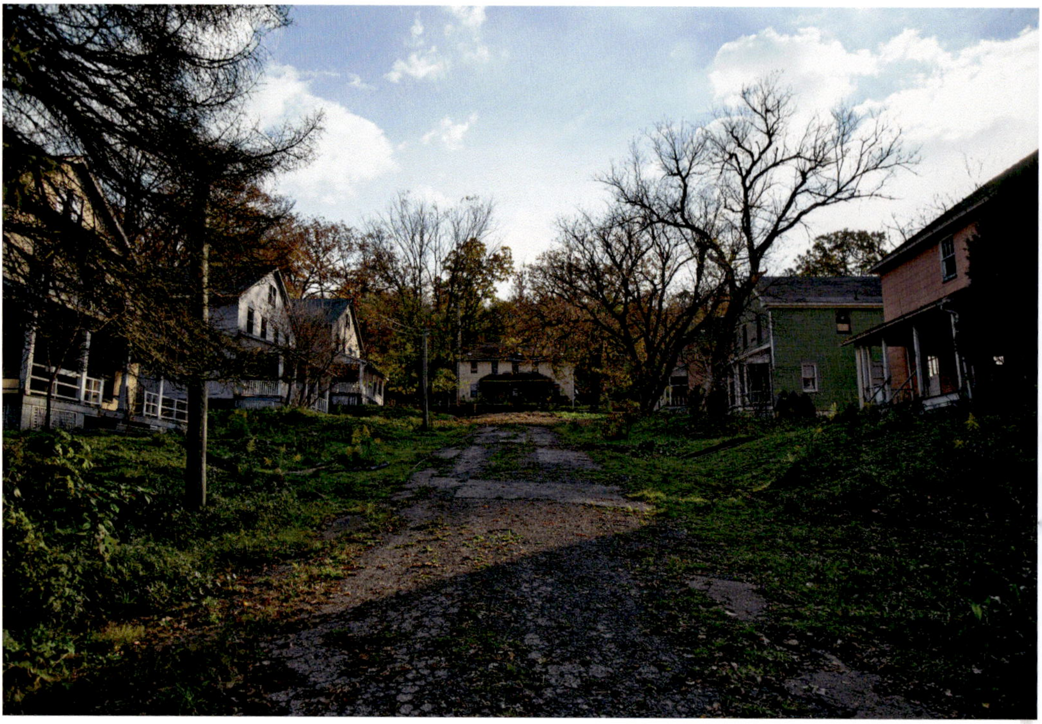

The sun was coming up over the abandoned street.

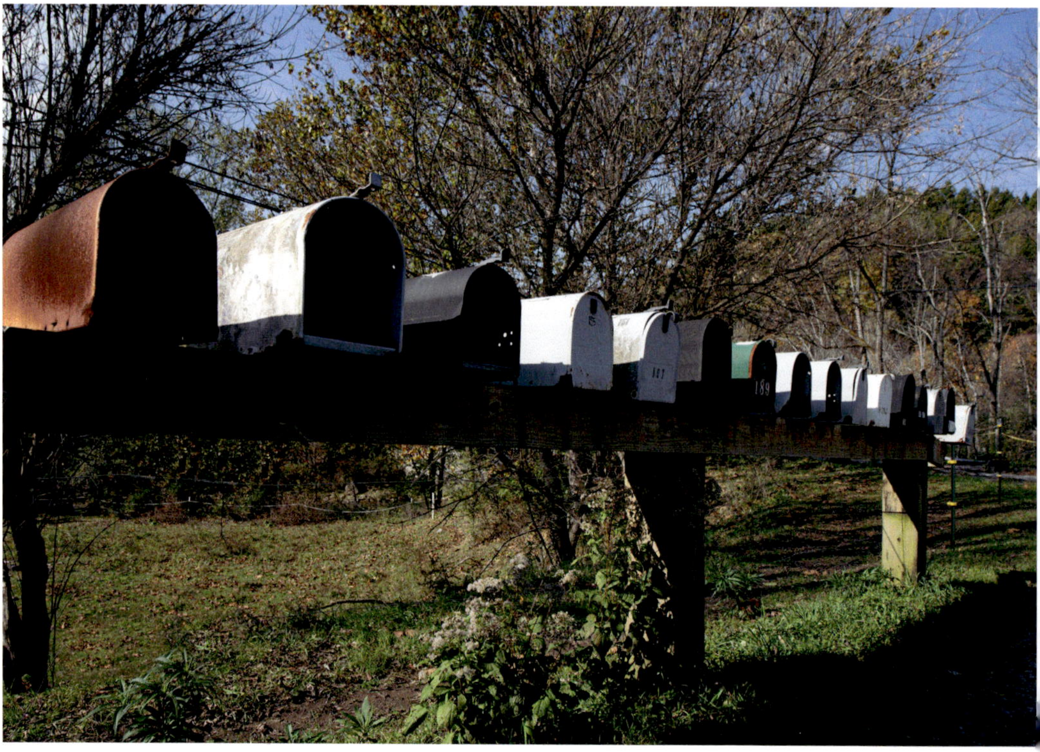

Empty mailboxes are still lined up on the main road in the village.